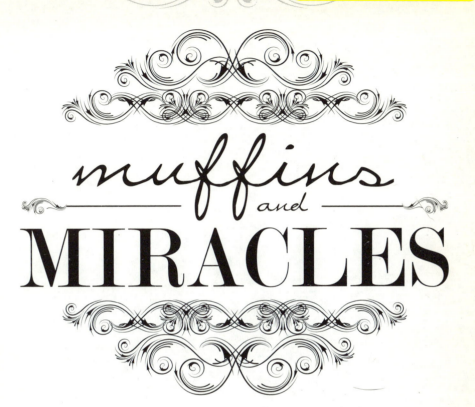

muffins *and* MIRACLES

muffins and MIRACLES

CHURCH SERVICE
— in the —
REAL WORLD

Compiled by

Linda Hoffman Kimball

CFI
AN IMPRINT OF CEDAR FORT, INC.
SPRINGVILLE, UTAH

ISBN 13: 978-1-4621-1126-8

Published by CFI, an imprint of Cedar Fort, Inc.
2373 W. 700 S., Springville, UT 84663
Distributed by Cedar Fort, Inc., www.cedarfort.com

LIBRARY OF CONGRESS CATALOGING-IN-PUBLICATION DATA

Kimball, Linda Hoffman, compiler.
Muffins & miracles : church service in the real world / Linda Hoffman Kimball.
    pages cm
Includes bibliographical references.
Summary: Women from varied life circumstances and church experience share their stories and insights about church service.
ISBN 978-1-4621-1126-8
1. Mormon women--Conduct of life. 2. Relief Society (Church of Jesus Christ of Latter-day Saints) 3. Church work--Church of Jesus Christ of Latter-day Saints. I. Title.

BX8643.W66K53 2013
248.4'893082--dc23

2012043975

Cover design by Rebecca J. Greenwood
Cover design © 2013 Lyle Mortimer
Typeset by Breanna L. Trost
Edited by Emily S. Chambers

Printed in the United States of America

10 9 8 7 6 5 4 3 2 1

This book is dedicated to
Evelyn Bee Kimball
(1929–2012)
who served and led and loved

Other books by
Linda Hoffman Kimball

Compiler:

Saints Well-Seasoned: Musings on How Food Nourishes
Us—Body, Heart, and Soul
Chocolate Chips and Charity: Visiting Teaching
in the Real World
Raspberries and Relevance: Enrichment
in the Real World
Apple Pies and Promises: Motherhood
in the Real World

Author:

Home to Roost
The Marketing of Sister B
Come with Me on Halloween
Enriching Ideas from A to Z

Contents

Contents

Introduction

SINCE THE EARLIEST days of the Restoration of the gospel of Jesus Christ, Church members have offered their time and talents to the building up of the kingdom of God on earth. Women and men of God serve, teach, visit, and lead each other. They do this to increase faith; strengthen homes; honor covenants; steward the privileges, blessings, and gifts of the priesthood; and to save souls. Concerning women's participation in this undertaking, Barbara W. Winder, eleventh Relief Society General President, counseled that unity is "not simply a matter of the sisters working together, but that we are partners with the priesthood brethren. We are companions in the work."[1]

In this era when more and more people are curious about the Church, many ask, "How can women be 'companions' or 'partners' if only the males are on the highest governing bodies of your organization?" This is a fair—and complex—question. There are many answers, none of them satisfying to everyone.

Christ has strong things to say about the balance between

service, leadership, and the exercise of authority. Matthew 20 shares this episode:[2] When the "mother of Zebedee's children" came to Jesus, angling for her two Apostle sons to sit on His right and left in His eventual kingdom, Jesus found himself teaching yet again. He gathered all of His Apostles together and explained that the world's way of running things—with the high-ranking and prestigious people "exercising dominion over" everyone else—was not God's way. Jesus explains, "But it shall not be so among you; but whosoever will be great among you, . . . let him be your servant."

Service and leadership are inextricably intertwined. Wherever we serve and lead, we are sisters and brothers in Christ. Female and male, our common aim as "committed disciples" (as Julie B. Beck, the fifteenth Relief Society General President, called us,[3]) is to further God's work on the earth. Whether pianist or prophet, presiding officer or Primary teacher, Christ inviteth them all to come unto him and partake of his goodness; and he denieth none that come unto him, black and white, bond and free, male and female; and he remembereth the heathen; and all are alike unto God.[4]

As President Dieter F. Uchtdorf of the First Presidency said, the goals of *all* who serve are to

> emulate the Savior, who, though a king, did not seek position, nor was He concerned about whether others noticed Him. He did not bother to compete with others. His thoughts were always tuned to help others. He taught, healed, conversed, and listened to others. He knew that greatness had little to do with outward signs of prosperity or position. He taught and lived by this doctrine: "He that is greatest among you shall be your servant."[5]

In one of the earliest Relief Society meetings on April 28, 1842, Joseph Smith underscored God's view of service and cautioned not to "consider the lower offices in the Church dishonorable and to look with jealous eyes upon the standing of others." This, he said, "was the nonsense of the human heart, for a person to be aspiring to other stations than appointed of God."[6] This "nonsense of the human heart" is what Christ expects "shall not be so among" us.[7]

The scriptures are full of powerful paradoxes. In them we learn that to save our lives we must lose them, and that the last shall be first. Requiring that our leadership be circumscribed in service is a paradox as well. On the one hand, it is clear that leadership should not be about status, jockeying for position or acclaim; on the other, we are promised that by living lives of service focused on Christ, our future will be replete with nobility and glories. Elder Russell M. Nelson of the Quorum of the Twelve Apostles wrote: "A woman's richest rewards will come as she rises to fulfill her destiny as a devoted daughter of God. To all faithful Saints He has promised thrones, kingdoms, principalities, glory, immortality, and eternal lives. . . . That is the potential for women in The Church of Jesus Christ of Latter-day Saints. It is exalting, everlasting, and divine."[8]

In the real world, how do we balance this paradox? It's in the living of it—in wrestling with the challenges of leadership and service—that we approach a glimmer of understanding.

As Spencer W. Kimball said, "There is a power in [the Relief Society] that has not yet been fully exercised to strengthen . . . the kingdom of God—nor will it until both the sisters and the [brethren of the] priesthood catch the vision of Relief Society."[9]

In the words of a million kids in mini-vans, "Are we there yet?"

Have we all "caught that vision"?

If you want to get a sense of what leadership and service look and feel like to a cross section of Mormon women, read on. This volume, *Muffins & Miracles: Church Service in the Real World*, offers you the voices of women who are in the thick of real-world service and leadership in the Church. Women across a broad spectrum of LDS perspectives share their thoughts, experiences, in-depth explorations, pithy bits of wisdom, highlights, and a few "lowlights" on the topics of women's leadership and service in the Church. These varied voices share honest stories of dedication and perseverance, innovation, and quiet (or not-so-quiet) heroism. Their words reflect joys and struggles along the journey as well as descriptions of what goodness looks like. Each piece has its own nugget of wisdom; collectively they reveal much about Latter-day Saint women in today's world.

While the list of contributors shows the names of many writers, others have preferred to use pseudonyms for privacy for all involved. (Their alter-egos were crafted from the names of some of the Church's illustrious founding mothers.)

We invite you to take in their words with open eyes, ears, and hearts. Welcome to this important conversation.

—Linda Hoffman Kimball
Evanston, IL, and Woodland, UT

PEOPLE OF POWER
Kate Holbrook

LATELY I HAVE been thinking about what I would like to give my daughters for when they are grown. The phrase that has come to mind most often as an answer is "a sense of their own power." By this I mean the kind of power they can have when they're living righteously with God and allowing God to be in their lives.

The word *power* is a complicated one because it has positive connotations—priesthood power, the power that created the earth, the power of God—and it also has negative connotations—"absolute power corrupting absolutely."

As part of my job (specialist in women's history for the Church History Department), I met with Sister Julie Beck, who was at the time the General Relief Society President. I asked her a version of my question concerning my daughters. "What would you like the women of Relief Society, the women of the Church, to have?"

She said, "When I think of that, words come to mind. Strength. Capacity. Purpose."

She said that women of the Church have these attributes.

In a BYU devotional talk, Elder James E. Faust addressed what his hopes are for his granddaughters—and all women in the Church:

> I do not want to tell you what you must be. That is for each
> of you to decide. You have your agency. Each of you will have
> to work very hard to learn all you can and develop your skills.
> It will not be easy to achieve anything really worthwhile. I
> want only to tell you what I think will help bring you identity,

sense of value, and happiness as a person. I also want to challenge you to reach your potential, to become a person of great worth, to become a great woman.

To me *great* does not necessarily mean your becoming a great doctor, lawyer, or business executive. You may, of course, become any of these if you so desire, and if you work hard enough, and I would be proud of such an achievement. However, to me, greatness is much, much more. I hope that each of you girls will become an individual of significant worth and a person of virtue so that your contributions are maintained in both human and eternal terms.[10]

These are great images for women. It seems that none of us thinks "Oh, we hope that you will just get by. We hope that you will have a mediocre life."

I want my daughters to have a sense of what they're good at, to know what their spiritual, emotional, and social resources are and to be able to fulfill some of their potential and feel God's pleasure as they do.

Right now I'm studying nineteenth-century early Mormon women. When I think about women who fulfilled their potential, Eliza R. Snow comes to mind. She helped establish the Relief Society in Nauvoo and to re-establish Relief Society in Utah. Brigham Young called her to travel to each ward to teach the bishop and the sisters what Relief Society should look like and how it should be. She directed all kinds of ideas for the Church and the women in the Church. She would talk over new initiatives with the president of the Church, Brigham Young, then John Taylor. She wanted to start sending women to medical school in the East. The women went and when they came back, they established a hospital called the Deseret Hospital.

Emmeline B. Wells was a nineteenth-century LDS woman who dealt with a lot of tragedy in her life. Some of her children died young, and some of the children who lived made bad choices and hurt one another. She just kept working hard, staying close to the Lord, and letting Him direct her to fulfill a divine destiny.[11] She was the secretary in the General Relief Society Presidency and later General Relief Society president.[12] For thirty-seven years she was the editor of *The Women's Exponent* magazine, which helped women all over the Church. *The Women's Exponent* reached sisters who were living in Hawaii or London or in places where the Church was new and where the members felt distanced from Zion. *The Women's Exponent* helped them know exactly what was going on and how they could run Relief Society in their own wards.

What *diminishes* our sense of power, strength, capacity, and purpose? Fear does. Fear stops our sense of God being with us, of doing what we need to do. It stops it in its tracks. I'm not saying you're a bad person if you have fear. We all have fear. What I am suggesting is that we practice rejecting fear.

Another thing that holds us back is a sense of having limited agency—a sense that we have no choice. A lot of times we think that we're in a situation where we don't have a choice in the matter. We always have a choice, and we're accountable for our choices.

Joseph Smith gave six talks to the Relief Society over the two years before he died in 1844. He taught the sisters about agency. He said: "After this instruction, you will be responsible for your own sins; it is a desirable honor that you should so walk before our Heavenly Father as to save yourselves; we are all responsible to God for the manner we improve the light and wisdom given by our Lord to enable us to save ourselves."[13]

To develop Godly strength and power, women need to be active agents of choice and accountable for the choices they make. Passivity is not suited to our best selves.

A third component that keeps us from sensing God's presence is sin. Disobedience. So avoid fear; remember that you have choices; try not to sin.

What can *help* us feel this capacity and strength? Faith can. Ezra Taft Benson said: "Men and women who turn their lives over to God will find out that He can make a lot more out of their lives than they can. He will deepen their joys, expand their vision, quicken their minds, strengthen their muscles, lift their spirits, multiply their blessings, increase their opportunities, comfort their souls, raise up their friends, and pour out peace."[14]

Joseph Smith established a Church where the worship services require people to develop their talents. Sometimes I wish we were able to hear a prepared, professional talk every week, but we don't get that. We get each other. We even teach our youngest children to pray and give talks in front of people. These practices stretch us out of our comfort zone and make us stronger, more powerful people.

I know strong women, and they inspire me. They make me want to develop my talents more. There's a real difference in being a powerful woman who is close to God. My wish for all of us is that we will have faith and confidence, and that we will be able to realize our strengths, our capacity, and our power as children of God, fulfilling our potential and feeling God's pleasure as we do.

MINISTRY
Ganie B. DeHart

ONE OF MY cousins is a Presbyterian minister. In many ways, she's more like me than any other member of my extended family, and I've sometimes wondered what it would be like to have her job. Actually, many aspects of her work are probably not all that different from my own teaching and counseling job. A few years ago, I realized that if I weren't

Mormon, I might feel called to the ministry, and I felt a bit sad that this option wasn't open to me. Then it occurred to me that—*because* I'm Mormon—I *am* called to minister. We're *all* called to minister, by virtue of promises made at baptism ("to bear one another's burdens") and in the temple. No matter what assignments we currently have at church, no matter what labels are placed on our service, we all have that same basic assignment: to minister to each other.

A SIMPLE MIRACLE
Connie Susa

HAVING SENT THE Church's *Faith in Every Footstep* DVD to Rhode Island's largest newspaper in the hope of spurring coverage for our pioneer sesquicentennial, I was pleased to hear the religion editor's voice when I answered the phone. I was, however, distressed to hear that he was up against a hard deadline.

He had several questions to round out a column dedicated to our pioneer heritage, but my instructions as stake public affairs director were that I must not speak for the Church. The only people whose answers could be reported by the media were priesthood holders of high office such as bishops and stake presidents. I promised to find someone whom he could quote, but he insisted that he had little time. He could only give me fifteen minutes to locate a spokesperson, and then he would phone me back.

Our own bishop was unavailable—out of town; our stake president lived across the Connecticut state line, so his opinions were automatically discounted for our state newspaper.

Even though most the other officials would still be at work in the late afternoon, I telegraphed a quick prayer and started down the list. I watched the minutes tick down as I reached answering machine after dismissive teen after chatty spouse. Just time enough for one more call, but who? "Father, please help me find the person You want to speak on Your behalf."

As I was about to dial the member of the stake presidency who lived in the Rhode Island half of our stake, the doorbell rang. I glanced out the side window in the living room to see Bishop Eric Fasteson from a neighboring ward standing at our kitchen door. Fourteen minutes had elapsed since I cradled the receiver from my phone call with our religion editor. I hurried to the door and said, "Bishop, I am so glad you came. The phone is going to ring, and it will be for you."

The bishop looked startled and held out a stack of temple preparation manuals, starting to explain that my husband had requested them several weeks earlier, and then the phone rang. As I moved toward the ringing, I explained in short bursts.

Bishop Fasteson is the patriarch of a large family, who live on a farm in the western edge of our state. Perhaps from such necessity, he has always been a calm man who keeps his statements simple and practical, one of "the strong, silent type." Instead of the spare answers I expected to hear from his side of the conversation, I heard profound truth with an inspired and almost poetic air. I heard the bishop's voice herald a celestial message.

We chatted briefly when his interview ended. He was again the Bishop Fasteson I had always known. He was concerned that he hadn't been able to name someone from our area who had a pioneer heritage. He hadn't felt any special prompting to deliver the needed manuals that particular afternoon. But he did acknowledge, "The Lord's hand was in it."

When the lengthy coverage appeared the following weekend, graced even further by the Church's professional graphics, it was easy to recognize that Bishop Fasteson and I had been the privileged instruments of our Heavenly Father's will.

PROXY
Alyson Beytien

WHEN OUR THREE sons were just four, three, and two, we received the diagnoses from specialists that all three of them were on the autism spectrum. We were so caught up in our stress over the boys that I'm not sure we were even aware of how the ward reacted initially. I'm sure there were many members who figured out that something was deeply wrong with our guys.

I told the Relief Society president, a close friend, about wanting to do a particular kind of therapy with the boys, but we couldn't afford it. She came to me one night and said that the ward wanted to help us do the therapy. I resisted vehemently, but eventually she wore me down.

The ward members signed up to help us do the therapy and receive all the training. Ten people went to sixteen hours of training and committed to eight hours a week of therapy with us. It was amazing, humbling, and difficult to accept the service. We were at a stage where we couldn't hold callings; attending Church was iffy at best; and still they helped. We had some truly touching, wonderful experiences in that situation.

One instance in particular was life-changing for me. It was the first full training session for Josh, our middle child, and the team of volunteer therapists. The "official" trainers were in town from California, and we were all sitting in the room, watching as each person practiced with Josh. He was not happy at all. He was screaming and hysterical, resistant to our instruction. It was taking everything I had not to break down and tell everyone to get out of my house and announce that I was not going to do this anymore. But I knew that if Josh saw me cry, he would never comply, and we would never make progress.

After maybe two people had their turn, it was one woman's turn to work with Josh. She started crying, looked at me, and said, "I can't do this. He's just so beautiful, and I feel his pain." She cried silently for about thirty seconds, and then got up and left.

She gave me such a gift that day because she cried when I couldn't. (Of course, I'm crying now as I write this!) She did not do the therapy with the boys, but she sent me cards, watched the other boys while I did the therapy, and found other ways to support. But her greatest service was stepping in and crying for me that day.

VOICES TO AFGHANISTAN
Carol Lynn Pearson

LIKE MILLIONS OF others around the globe, I had watched the worsening situation in Afghanistan—especially for the women—with sadness and outrage. No access to education! What could we possibly do for them?

About the time the Taliban fell, in the fall of 2001, I had an idea. And because I am a diary-keeper, I know that it came on Friday night, November 16.

"*I hardly slept. I got an idea just as I was pulling up my covers, and it wouldn't let me go. It got bigger and bigger. Even when I finally slept, I kept coming in and out of consciousness developing it."*

What if we could give to our friends in Afghanistan . . . our language! Not that English is superior to Farsi, but it happens to be the international language, and the better people can communicate, the stronger the bridges of understanding, trust, and opportunity.

What if we could collect hundreds, thousand of basic books in English—children's picture books would be perfect!—and send them to the schools in Afghanistan? Wait! What if we could help them by reading those books to them! What if thousands of people each sent a personal gift of his or her voice, reading aloud on tape the book they are donating! What if they taped inside the book a photo of themselves, along with their personal statement!

By morning, I was exhausted but exhilarated. That very day I wrote a letter proposing the project to several large organizations that I felt could help execute it, but my efforts were not successful.

However, a year and a half later, I accepted the calling to serve on the Oakland Stake Public Affairs Council. On my first meeting with the Council, our excellent and newly-appointed leaders, Gary and Lynn Anderson, outlined clearly what our mission was. "We are here to find ways for the members of the Church to go out into the community and serve," Gary said. "Let's put our ideas on the table. Carol Lynn, why don't you go first? You just want to save the world, don't you?"

"Absolutely," I replied. "And as a matter of fact, I've got an idea."

Ten minutes later, the Council was on fire with the possibilities of extending ourselves in such a personal way to our brothers and sisters in Afghanistan. A few months later, over 800 books and tapes had been collected from the members of the stake, some of their neighbors, a few schools and scout troops in the area. We had established "Voices to Afghanistan" as an independent, non-profit foundation. We had raised enough money for the purchase of tape players for at least fifty schools. We had developed a relationship with the "Afghanistan Relief Organization" to assist in transporting the books and getting them to the schools.

I wish I could give a detailed report of how tremendously successful this project was, but I can't. We had vastly underestimated the problems of communication in that chaotic country. All I know for sure is that the books and tapes from our stake and hundreds of subsequent donations made their way to Afghanistan. And I hope and believe that many of them reached minds and hearts there and said, "Here is a good wish from a friend in America. Here is a story and here is my voice."

MERCIFUL CALLINGS
Tania Rands Lyon

I AM A CONTROL freak and don't usually do well with surprises. Thankfully, the Lord has been willing to work with this particular weakness now and then. As a newlywed, my husband and I lived in a small ward in a rural area where Church leaders were spread thin. I was called into the Young Women presidency and enjoyed teaching the Beehives. The Young Women president, however, was preparing to have a baby, and the writing was on the wall that she would likely need to be replaced within a few months. I felt far from presidential material and liked my supporting role, so I never considered myself a candidate.

One day, as I sat in our apartment immersed in writing my dissertation, computer keys tapping away, I felt a shaft of light or heat or *something* permeate my body from the top of my head downward and was immediately filled with an awareness that I was to be the next Young Women president. No voice, no thunder—just pure knowledge. I remember my hands frozen above the keyboard as I absorbed this revelation. It was several more months before the call came, but thanks to a kind and merciful God, I was ready when it did.

LESSONS FROM THE LAMBS[15]
Linda Hoffman Kimball

I HAVE A NEW Church calling. This one has the unusual perk of two hours a week of kissing and hugging.

I'm a nursery worker. Back when I was a stay-at-home mom raising my own tots (who are now adults), this was the calling I most dreaded and, thankfully, never got. Motherhood was so unrelenting. It was a challenge to stay intellectually engaged. And pats on the back? I was the only one dishing those out through my arduous, insecure trek through the Desert of No Immediate Rewards.

But now that I have some years and experience on me, I'm up for this weekly love-and-germ fest. Our ward has thirty-six kids between the ages of eighteen months and three years. They are divided into "older" and "younger" nurseries, and I'm assigned to the eighteen young ones. We have an enlightened leadership. We have a staff that includes male workers, allows practical clothing, and is passionate about not making this time just about "babysitting."

My first Sunday, the leader of the younger nursery explained the nuts and bolts of our job. Our main tasks consist of (1) being a mediator (to intervene or to redirect energies before somebody gets konked on the head), and (2) being a soother. As I thought about that during the week, my mind segued from "mediator" to "the Great Mediator" and from "soother" to "the Comforter." Is there another Church calling where those Godly functions get such direct application?

I spent most of my time that first day holding the bishop's child. She has adorable black curls and bright eyes and is one plump presence. She's the youngest of the young nursery bunch and is still transitioning. At one point, she was clinging to my neck while I stooped down to pick up another crying tyke.

With my age and experience have come bad knees, so getting up from a squat with thirty-pound weeping weights on each hip was more than I could balance. The other nursery workers helped the unit of us three up, and all was well. Both kids stopped crying, and I felt like I was channeling primal feminine power of the most blessed sort. As my quads ached throughout the week, I recognized this calling even included a fitness plan.

In the nursery, our littlest lambs tend to choose women to run to for cuddling, consoling, hugging, or lifting up. Before we wander into sexist stereotyping, I will also add that most of the girls spent good chunks of time hammering at the tool bench with hard hats on, and almost all the boys were dazzled by the Fischer Price vanity counter with rotating mirror.

In my early motherhood days, of course I loved my own kids beyond measure. But in that constant vigilance, parts of me seemed to leech away. Now that I'm pretty much reconstituted, I'm thrilled to give back. I'm glad to provide a little respite for the young parents out there who, like I did, really appreciate and need it. I'm delighted to shower love on—and absorb wonder from—these tiny people. I'm pleased to relearn action songs—including that one grown-ups sing, unaware of the literal aerobic benefits:

> *More fit for the kingdom, More used would I be,*
> *More blessed and holy—More, Savior, like thee.*[16]

THE WELCOME MAT
L. Y. Robison

W HAT'S THAT WELCOME mat? I don't remember a welcome mat at the back door when I toured the apartment with the building manager. But then, I breezed through the apartment so quickly before I told the manager "I'll take it!" that maybe I just missed a few details like the welcome mat. I mean, what's to think long and hard about? Bedroom, kitchen, bathroom, living room, one-and-a-half closets—sounded like all the essentials.

The fresh carpet and new tub hinted at a landlord who's likely to take care of the place. It was a perfect location—a quiet neighborhood of well-kept, small yards. An apartment of my own. Looked like a safe place. Two keys—one for the outer door and one for my apartment door—added an extra level of security.

Friday night, driving home from work, the swish of the windshield wipers punctuated my thoughts. It was the first time all week that I slowed down long enough to think. Are things really that bad to justify this drastic step? Have I really tried everything possible to rescue the marriage? Could I make it on my own—financially and emotionally? What made me think I *could* live alone when I'd always had parents, brothers, roommates, children, or a husband to live with, every single year of my life? Was no relationship at all truly better than a bad one? And, naming the biggest fear of all, could I survive the crushing daily loneliness that I'd just served up for myself? The questions kept coming, faster than I could even begin to formulate answers.

I just knew what I had to do.

Driving through the rain, I made my way toward the old house to sleep one last time. My soon-to-be ex was safely out of town for the weekend, which made my moving out easier for both of us. We'd already agreed which furniture I'd be taking with me; it would be enough to get me started.

Since I was at work all day, I didn't have time to clean the new apartment myself. I gave my extra key to two Relief Society sisters, asking them if they could do a quick once-over before I moved in.

On the way to the old house, I stopped at my empty apartment to give it one last check. I folded up my umbrella and climbed the two flights of stairs. That's when I noticed the unfamiliar but cheery welcome mat. After wiping my soggy shoes on the mat, I turned the key in the lock.

A bright-yellow mum plant greeted me on a deep rust-tinted tablecloth, draped over a table I'd never seen before. How did they know I would need a kitchen table? Blonde wood chairs, print placemats, and carved wooden napkin rings (napkin rings!) completed the table setting. Hand soap, tissues, wastebaskets, toilet paper, light bulbs, and paper towels were sprinkled throughout the apartment like fairy dust that landed in all the right places.

The extra key lay on the counter.

COUNTING SHEEP
Nancy Harward

Jesus saith to Simon Peter, Simon son of Jonas, lovest thou me more than these? He saith unto him, Yea, Lord; thou knowest that I love thee. He saith unto him, Feed my lambs.

He saith to him again the second time, Simon, son of Jonas, lovest thou me? He saith unto him, Yea, Lord; thou knowest that I love thee. He saith unto him, Feed my sheep.

He saith unto him the third time, Simon, son of Jonas, lovest thou me? Peter was grieved because he said unto him the third time, Lovest thou me? And he said unto him, Lord, thou knowest all things; thou knowest that I love thee. Jesus saith unto him, Feed my sheep. (John 21:15–17)

THE PAST MONTH had been particularly hectic. I recently began a part-time job—my first experience working as a paid employee in over sixteen years—and I was still trying to figure out how to fit everything I normally did into a week that had suddenly become twenty-four hours shorter. I struggled to keep the refrigerator stocked, serve dinner before bedtime, and prevent piles of dirty laundry from entirely blocking the entrance to the bathroom. The seeds I had intended to get in the ground as soon as all danger of frost was past were still sealed in their packets, and now it was May. May is the month when all parents of school-age children are expected to devote one-third of their waking hours to helping their kids complete final projects and prepare for exams, and another one-third to attending those endless sports banquets, band concerts, chorus concerts, dance recitals, awards assemblies, and class picnics that teachers seem to think are indispensable at the end of the school year.

Late each night, I would collapse into bed, totally exhausted, yet unable to sleep. Counting sheep did not help at all. In fact, counting sheep was what kept me awake. In addition to being a working mother, I was a Relief Society president, and I was worried about the flock the Lord had entrusted to me. A tornado had ravaged our community a few weeks earlier, and several ward members were either looking for new homes or trying to repair damaged ones. Many others had been devastated emotionally, if not physically.

Even before the tornado, our Relief Society had included more than a few women with disabilities, risky pregnancies, shaky marriages, defiant children, inadequate financial resources, and fragile testimonies—tender lambs in need of a watchful shepherd. It was probably an average caseload for an average ward, but for me, it was overwhelming. I was ready to throw in my crook.

On the first Sunday in May, I went to Welfare Committee meeting reluctantly, afraid of the questions the bishop might ask and ashamed of the answers I must give:

Is someone checking on Sister S (a distraught tornado victim) every few days?

I hope so.

Have visiting teachers been assigned to Sister W (a new convert)?

Not yet.

What has been done to help Sister G (an elderly widow who could no longer care for herself) find another place to live?

I don't know.

The bishop, however, did not ask any questions. Instead, he looked at the members of the Welfare Committee seated around the room and said, "It's been a particularly hectic month. No doubt most of you have felt like I have, overwhelmed by the number of things we could be doing to help the people we're supposed to help and feeling a little guilty that we haven't gotten around to all of them. It seems like no matter how much we do, there's always more that could be done. But before we start beating ourselves up about what we haven't done this month, let's look at what we *have*. I think you'll find it's a pretty amazing list.

"We've put a new roof on the M's house. We've cleared several yards of fallen trees and other debris. We've helped relocate at least three households. Our youth have sorted food at the relief center. Our members have been angels of mercy to dozens of their neighbors and friends."

He went on. "We've witnessed a family being sealed in the temple. We've shared the gospel with our coworkers. We've expressed love for each other and taught our children the meaning of service. We've seen testimonies grow."

I left Welfare Committee meeting that morning much less discouraged than I had gone in. In Relief Society, I was able to present the lesson I had prepared—a message about feeding hungry sheep—with a spirit of hope, not desperation. Later that afternoon, I reflected on what the bishop had said, and began to enumerate good things I knew our Relief Society sisters had accomplished in the past few weeks. I was grateful for dependable counselors, who had kept the organization running while I struggled to find a balance between my regular responsibilities and my new job. I was grateful for a dedicated Compassionate Service leader, who had cheerfully, faithfully, and effectively fulfilled every assignment she was given. I appreciated diligent visiting teachers who had recognized needs that I never even saw and took care of them.

As I sat thinking about the ways that members of our ward had served and blessed each other, I became conscious that I had been humming a certain melody over and over for several minutes. All of a sudden, I realized what tune it was. It was a song from *White Christmas*, a movie I hadn't seen or thought of for years. But in my mind, I could hear Bing Crosby singing:

If you're worried and you can't sleep,
Just count your blessings instead of sheep.
And you'll fall asleep
Counting your blessings.[17]

That night, for the first time in several weeks, I slept very well.

THIS ISN'T GIRLS' CAMP
Kelly Austin

THE LIGHT FILTERED down through the trees, casting a golden hue. Any other day, this would have been a serene setting—tall, faithful trees; a cool breeze; rugged, beautiful cliffs. Today, the serenity was interrupted by the shouts and cheers of about a dozen twelve- to eighteen-year-old girls: "Go, Fatimah!" "You're almost there, Kyme!" "I'm so proud of you, Leah." "You can do it, Angie!"

It was my first summer as Young Women president, and I had no camp counselor—well, more like I was my *own* camp counselor. I grew up in a family of Boy Scouts: my dad was always the Scout master, and my three brothers all received their Eagle Scout awards. I remember watching them leave for amazing adventures: mountain climbing, Philmont, rappelling, white water rafting.

And each year, for Girls' Camp, I packed up and went to some nearby Kansas wheat field for campfire songs and crafts. Don't get me wrong: I usually had fun with my friends—and definitely felt the love and care of my leaders. But something in me wasn't content with the disparity between my experience and my brothers'. When I was called to Young Women, I knew

I wanted to give the girls the camp experience I'd never had.

When the girls and I arrived at the camp in the hills of Ohio, we ran into two other LDS units camping nearby. When I mentioned that I was taking our girls rock climbing and rappelling, the other leaders looked at me, shocked, and asked, "How did you get your bishop to agree to that?" I had to laugh—it had never occurred to me to ask permission. And, fortunately, he didn't seem to think I needed to ask permission either. When I told our bishop my plans for camp, he simply nodded, agreed, and asked to be a part of it.

Once at camp, I knew that I had to join the girls in both the rock climbing and the rappelling. I couldn't, after all, let a bunch of Beehives show me up. First, I climbed to the top of the rock-climbing crevice and then walked to the top of the mountain and rappelled from the edge of the nearby cliff. It certainly wasn't graceful (I hit the last rock with my rear end instead of my feet), but I did it.

One of the other leaders, Gail, was also determined to give rappelling a try despite her intense fear of heights. She was not, to say the least, a classic camper. Each night in the leaders' tent, we had to conduct a search for spiders and kill them. The Great Outdoors was not her thing—a contrast to another leader, who was determined to use her wilderness skills by digging her own bathroom trench on our hike. But we were in this for the girls.

As Gail descended the edge of the cliff for her rappel, she hesitated—multiple times. Caught up in the moment, I was cheering her on—or egging her on—not realizing her real terror. The bishop, a bit more prescient in that moment, took off running up the path to the top. Minutes later, they came down the cliff face, side by side, the bishop talking to her all the way down. Gail was shaking as she reached the bottom, but there was a sense of pride in conquering her fear—and a resolve to never, *ever* face that fear again.

I watched that day as each girl reached the bottom of her rappel or the top of her climb. The reactions varied: some cried, some cheered, some shook uncontrollably, some sunk to their knees, and some walked away nonchalantly. I'll never forget watching one young woman as she landed from her rappel: "I am never doing *that* again," she insisted. But as her friend remarked that her example had given her courage to try the rappel herself, this same young women replied, "Then I'll go with you. We'll do it together." And off they ran.

I'm not sure I made many converts to rock climbing that day. But each of us—leader, bishop, or young woman—had conquered something—a fear, a goal, or a mere mountain—and the joy of that conquest was possible through the love, encouragement, and support of each other.

As we were eating lunch later, one of the older girls, a bit of a tomboy, looked at me and exclaimed, "This isn't Girls' Camp!" I must have looked a bit perplexed, so she continued, "No, this is Scout Camp. Because *this* was cool!" I had to smile. I'd been thinking the same thing: this was certainly not the Girls' Camp of my youth. But it was the one I'd always dreamed of.

FLOAT HOPES
K. Carpenter

Since I couldn't come right out and ask my stake president, "What were you thinking?" I asked if I could have some time to consider the calling extended to me. The calling was to be in charge of our stake's assignment for a float to be entered in Salt Lake City's 24th of July parade next year

Float creation was definitely not on my resume in any

shape or form! Furthermore, in June of the float year, my husband and I were going to celebrate our fiftieth wedding anniversary by gathering our scattered family of thirty for a week, and that event would take considerable attention. In addition, I was pursuing answers to a collection of "vague neurological symptoms," which, though not life-threatening, were affecting the quality of my activities.

Within the next week, I returned to respond. Going into the office, I was prepared to decline, but I came out the door having accepted this extraordinary call much to my own amazement and my husband's consternation. There was no arm-twisting, pleading, or spiritual blackmail but just a quiet gift saying, "you can do this" and the faith of my stake presidency that indeed I *could* do this.

There was one other thing—the event was a year away, so I had plenty of time to gather what was needed, including my wits. Or so I thought.

First on my list was to ask "What is our purpose; why are we doing this?" What could be the reason behind the anxiety, labor, and expense needed to produce floats for parades? The official response from the presidency of the Seventy was, "It is important that Church members remember and reverence the sacrifice and dedication of those that first made the trek to this valley." I could agree with that reasoning. However, I inquired, was our stake looking to win an award, as several were available? Was that a secondary agenda?

I discovered most such prizewinners in the prior year went way over budget and collected donations to make up the difference—and with spectacular results. Such an approach did not sit well with me, but I would do the best job possible for the amount allotted to honor our heritage. Another thing: I was out of the loop since I had been caretaker for my mother for five years and consequently did not know many people in our stake. Obviously, I needed help.

The first course of action was to send out sign-up sheets to each ward. Amazingly these were returned with signatures of willing, talented volunteers.

Okay. So what next? The official parade theme for 2009 was "Utah's Pioneers: Catch the Vision," which we morphed into our concept, "Families United: Utah's Vision." Beginning thoughts centered on visualizing values that should be common between current and pioneer families. Aha! Our 37' x 12' float showcased a modern family up front, with a mom wrapped in a quilt reading to her daughter while her husband and son rototilled a colorful garden of corn, tomatoes, carrots, and flowers. In the rear, the pioneer mother sat quilting as her daughter tilled their crop of corn, squash, wheat, and flowers.

These families were separated by a giant handcart holding huge gardening tools, big "values" books, an enormous goofy dog (just for the fun factor) and a tall bolt of the quilts traversing from past to present (back to front of the float). Toss in some glittery sagebrush, foil fringe, fake grass, and a rocky road, and we were done. Viola!

Every Primary child was invited to add to a chorus of pioneer songs broadcast along the parade route which was an additional enhancement. All that was left was the hope that this creation could survive two parades—the 4th of July parade, which was a trial run, and the July 24th in Salt Lake City.

There were mini-miracles all along the way. To recognize just a few: Jane's artistic rendition turned vague ideas into a plan for action. Art let us build the float on his property, and he built the handcart—even finding authentic big wheels. Rosie came up with inexpensive, impressive costumes. Andrew A. invented the enormous, happy, furry dog. Andrew M. created, carved, and painted red rock side panels. Shauna and crew produced oversized, vibrant, glittering vegetables and amazing things of foam. PVC pipe works wonders too. There were professional welders in our stake who fashioned the form for the quilt bolt—our prime focal point—and anchored the many props and safety posts.

Who drives floats? They are basically an oversized, heavily laden platform mounted on an antique chassis. A willing, experienced crane driver came to the rescue. The immense quilt, which swirled across the entire float, was really seventy red, yellow, and blue crib-size quilts. We donated the quilts to the LDS Humanitarian Center when the float was dismantled.

Personal miracles were revealed in the efforts of Erin, my tireless co-chair, who handled many details and followed through and smoothed some miscommunication while being a mom and working part-time. "Assembly and Finishing" was the title for Boyd, our jack-of-all-trades, who endured to the end accomplishing every last pesky problem. He will probably never get spilled paint out of his truck bed. Boyd and his family also joined other families offering time and abilities. It was beautiful to behold them working together, able to do many needed tasks. Our own vacationing son and family arrived just in time to design, paint, and glue all sorts of stuff.

One "big" miracle came as a result of our float being misidentified. Floats are numbered for order in parade and judging. We had not been concerned about the judging other than following the rules for participation. However, a group of judges wandered by looking at the number that *had* been ours before a last-minute change. When we let them know of the change, they promptly informed us we had won the Legacy Award, "presented to the float that best illustrates the Legacy received from those who came before us," which had been the hope for our float all along. As one last hurrah, our float surprised us by showing up the next day in full color on the front page of the *Deseret News*. It was a very happy 24th of July!

And just so you know, Egg McMuffins fueled all the float folks before each parade run. We could not have done it without them!

We made budget—well, within $50.00, which went for all the McMuffins, of course.

Our float engine quit at Liberty Park, the parade route's end, which necessitated a tow of about eight miles ending at Boyd's home where a front tire promptly blew, and I mean BLEW!

Rather than seeing Relief Society as a noun—a place, a status, a class, a lesson, the "third hour"—we need to see the Relief Society as a verb. It is an action. When we do Relief Society, rather than attend a Relief Society meeting, we em-brace sisterhood and become servants of Christ. —Sherrie M. L. Gavin

---

"I WAS IN PRISON, AND YOU VISITED ME"
Connie Susa

WHEN I WORKED as the Parent Training Specialist for our state department of education, I heard that incarcerated women who were nearing their parole dates needed a variety of training and supports to help prepare them for reunification with their children.

I had never considered how difficult it must be to be judged

guilty in front of one's impressionable children. Furthermore, these children often feel abandoned by and alienated from their mothers. During their mother's absence, the children look to someone else (such as a grandmother or foster-care worker) as the nurturer and authority in their lives, and it is difficult for female prisoners to transition back into the roles that define parenthood or sometimes even to assume those roles for the first time.

Paroled mothers need to bond with and guide their children, while others (parole officers, social workers, the substitute caregivers, addiction counselors) watch the process. These "others" often expect to find failure, misinterpret, or don't give enough time for the efforts to take hold before instituting protective custody proceedings that would separate the family members again.

As I was introduced to the problems associated with reunification, I recognized for the first time that the difficult role of motherhood became substantially more complex and stressful under these circumstances. Nothing in the lexicon of our department of education parent trainings came close to addressing such issues.

However, my role as a trainer of trainers in the Church's Parent Education Training series offered wisdom that could be universally applied. Moreover, using the Church's Family Home Evening program weekly through the years had helped me recognize that to be effective, parenting must be purposeful. Our children are barraged many times every day with messages that attempt to degrade our family-centered lifestyle. Parents must actively work to transmit their values by precept and example. This was exactly what these women needed to carve a trusted place back in the lives of their children.

I approached our bishop with my concept for a training program inside the walls of our state's Adult Correctional Institution. He gave me approval and the names of several sisters I might recruit to do this with me, since this was not an official Church calling. One by one, sisters turned down "the opportunity." Hadn't they been reading the same scripture I had? "I was in prison and you visited me. . ."

Disappointed, but understanding the fears and other time commitments of my sisters, I submitted a proposal as an individual for a short training series that used no religious proselytizing, but focused entirely on the good parenting principles I had learned through the Church. The education board at the prison required a commitment that I would not even mention the name of the Church. I agreed and scheduled a date to begin.

When I entered the women's penitentiary for the first time, the gulf between my daily life and that of convicted women loomed before me. I explained my mission to the guard behind the bars and bullet-proof glass and provided my documentation. Normally, I would also have been searched, but "the greeter" was interrupted and just referred me to the activity room on the third floor. Metal doors clanged closed and locked behind me, and I was inside.

Accustomed to the experience of prison life and unaware that I was not, a guard on the third floor showed me to the designated room and stated that the six women would be joining me shortly. "Won't you be with me?" I asked. She shook her head.

"You mean I'll be alone?" My voice shook this time.

"You will be fine," she assured. "All these women are considered minimum security risks because they are within three months of their release date." She added that none of them had committed any violence while inside, and none of them wanted to jeopardize their release. They would come to my class and leave on their own.

The first prisoner entered and looked around. I noted her tough swagger and strong arms. My heart pounded. I introduced myself, shook hands with this stranger, and listened as she tried to assure me that she was a changed woman, that she wanted a clean and peaceful life with her children, that she was done with the people and substances that had gotten her into trouble. Each participant, in turn, introduced herself with similar assurances, guessing I was, perhaps, assessing them. I explained that I would be teaching parenting skills that I had learned from my church, and I launched the first lesson.

For the third lesson in my parenting series, I intended to run the class like a Family Home Evening lesson. I would instruct the group as if I were the mother and they were my children. Forbidden to bring refreshments into the prison, I would have to content myself with enlivening the lesson with stories, hands-on learning activities, "chalk-talk" discussion, and a little song. It would be fun to demonstrate how to convey moral principles to their children.

I picked an appropriate lesson from the Family Home Evening Manual, practiced it with my own family the Monday before, and assembled all the materials to teach the class. The women eagerly took on the role of children. Some had experienced shortened childhoods in one way or another and enjoyed the few moments to revisit a carefree time. However, the woman to my right didn't jostle or tease like the others. Instead, she tipped her head sideways to read the tiny lettering on the back cover of my manual. I turned it over to see what had attracted her studied gaze. The full name of the Church was printed there.

Remembering my commitment to the prison authorities, I assured her that I was not present in a missionary role, not trying to convert anyone in the group to our Church. "Oh, that's not why I was interested," she said. "I used to live right next door to your church."

"Really?" I was intrigued.

"Yeah," she said. "You guys bought my house from the state."

"I don't understand." It was more of an invitation for more, rather than a statement.

"Well, I lived in a drug house, so the state confiscated it," she said matter-of-factly. "Your church bought it, tore it down, and turned it into extra parking for all the cars on Sundays."

Shaken that such dangerous activities had gone on literally next door to me every week, I moved mechanically on with the lesson. The women thanked me at the end, but the revelation made me doubt that this neighbor or any of the other women could be ready in a few of my short lessons to lead their families into an ethical utopia.

I had designed the program as a secular teaching experience. At the department of education I had taught content and various facts. Here I was trying to teach new behaviors—more than discrete behaviors—a new lifestyle. Trying to change lives, trying to reach across that societal gulf with only my arms of flesh seemed suddenly overwhelming. When people self-select into the missionary lessons, they are often open to and converted by the Holy Spirit. I realized, for the first time, what it meant to have literally a captive audience, who had not chosen me and my message.

If I ever have the occasion again to replicate such a series behind prison walls, I will multiply the number of lessons, and, unlike a secular trainer, I will don the armor of faith through prayer and fasting.

ELISABETH'S FRIENDS[18]

Kristine Haglund

> Now Elisabeth's full time came that she should be delivered; and she brought forth a son. And her neighbours and her cousins heard how the Lord had shewed great mercy upon her; and they rejoiced with her. (Luke 1:57–58)

I'VE BEEN WONDERING about Elisabeth's neighbors. Surely among them were one or two who had also longed for children they couldn't have, to whom God had not shown the particular mercy he showed Elisabeth. It seems likely they would have been Elisabeth's closest friends, sharing the pain of what they called barrenness, puzzling over and understanding together the unfairness of what others attributed to God's cursing.

Did they join in the rejoicing? How? At what cost in choked-down grief and forced smiles and quick exits for private sobbing? I once hosted a baby shower for a friend about four hours after I had to have a post-miscarriage procedure. Going ahead with it seemed simpler than calling everyone and explaining what had happened. So I have some small idea whereof I speak.

Perhaps it is because this particular grief is one that seems omnipresent in a family-oriented Church, and so many of my friends are grappling with it, at the same time as many others of my friends are welcoming babies and the new set of struggles that arrives with each one. I wonder how to be one of Elisabeth's true friends, how to mourn with my friends who mourn while remaining ready to rejoice truly and deeply at the miracle of each birth.

For now, my woefully partial and inadequate solution is . . . knitting. I have a pile of half-finished baby blankets, and while I'm lousy at more conventional forms of prayer, I'm pretty good at thinking of my friends while I'm knitting and purling. And although I ordinarily don't think knitting in sacrament meeting is "proper," I always work on baby blankets on Sundays when babies are blessed. My friends know I am knitting for them, and it is a way to signal that I am remembering their hurt and doing the best I can to enter into it with them.

Strangely, graciously, it seems that as I stretch myself out in this tiny way, my puny attempts at charity have the effect of unraveling my own troubles, even when those troubles are not ameliorated in any tangible, obvious ways. This gives me hope that even though we can't make sense of the apparently random suffering and unrewarded righteous longings of latter-day Zacharias and Elisabeths, the mere attempt to live up to our baptismal covenants has real power to bind up our wounds—that "having our hearts knit together in love" can begin to heal the ragged edges of our variously broken hearts.

TRUE PIONEERS
Suzanne Midori Hanna

As RELIEF SOCIETY president, I had an insider's view of an historic time when missionaries were first sent to African-American neighborhoods. Although the priesthood revelation came in 1978, missionary work in our segregated city was just beginning to change in 1989. My second counselor, Gaye, was an avid genealogist and had traced her family back many generations. As African-American Saints began to enrich our ward family, a retired couple, Waverly and Joy, became new converts and instant friends with many of us in the ward. To our amazement, Gaye and Joy discovered a common last name. Gaye's great-great-grandfather had been a slave-holder in the area. Joy's grandmother was born from a slave and her master. They compared family records, names, and dates. They were cousins!

These two sisters—one white, one black—taught me how to have personal conversations about race within our ward family. Despite the legacy that might keep them apart, a common ancestor and the Church brought them together. I had visited the ward of other wonderful pioneers where many black converts had changed the demographics of their ward families. However, I had not lived that experience in my own ward until then.

I felt a tremendous stirring of love and inspiration within me as black and white sat down together each week in our ward. One white member said with pride, "You know, Martin Luther King used to say that Sunday was the most segregated day of the week!" We knew we were making history. There were so many converts that a third of our active members came from our black neighborhoods. Ironically, one weekend, while we were all in sacrament meeting together, the Ku Klux Klan was demonstrating on the county courthouse steps!

We felt the loving hand of the Lord as we came together and crossed the lines of race, culture, economics, and heritage. It was not always easy for our African-American members. They were still subjected to insensitive behavior from some in the majority and in leadership positions. They told me it was sometimes lonely for them to have leaders who didn't understand cultural issues. But many were able to withstand these injuries and hang in there. Today they are role models for others who come, who need the sense of belonging that all Saints deserve to have in the Church.

As the Relief Society president, I had to ask myself, "Who is leading whom?" I was changed forever by the courage, patience, and testimony of our members. Just as the pioneers of old, these modern-day pioneers "sang as they walked and walked and walked and walked and walked." ·

DIVINE INTERVENTION
Nancy Harward

I DIDN'T WANT TO teach seminary for the simple reason that I knew it would be hard. Maybe even impossible. To begin with, I was not a morning person, and in our ward, seminary began at 5:50 a.m. Then there was the fact that I was neither an awe-inspiring scriptorian nor an awesome entertainer. Nevertheless, I knew—as surely as I had known that my husband would become our next bishop—that I was to become the next seminary teacher.

I'd had the premonition for months, realizing that once my husband became bishop, I would have to be released as Relief Society president and thus would be "free" to teach seminary. The feeling had been so strong and so persistent that it had driven me to spend a lot of time on my knees pleading with the Lord to make it go away. But in the end, I had submitted. I told Heavenly Father: "I don't want to teach seminary, but if you really want me to, I will—as long as you're there to help."

Having submitted, I was blessed with an assurance that I could quit worrying about it. Although the current seminary teacher had been serving for six years, there was no reason she couldn't continue. Sister Woods loved the kids, and the kids loved her. Besides, any new seminary teacher would have

36

to be recommended by the bishop, and my husband knew better than anyone how un-awesome and how not a morning person I was. So the dread of seminary was dispelled from my mind—until the newly sustained bishop informed me that he had called Sister Woods to be the new Relief Society president. With the seminary year set to begin in less than two weeks, I suddenly felt as though I'd been pushed off a cliff. "So who's going to teach seminary?" I asked. "You're not going to recommend *me*, are you?"

My husband must have missed the trepidation in my voice because he laughed as though he thought I was joking. "I know better than to do *that!*" he said. "But how would you feel about being the ward in-service leader?"

I thought I would feel tremendously relieved to be the ward in-service leader, but, curiously, I didn't. I accepted the call, but it never felt right. I served without enthusiasm. One might almost say that I served grudgingly, because I wasn't sure the call had come from the Lord.

Meanwhile, Paul North had been assigned to teach seminary. Paul was a newly married graduate student who had just moved into our ward, and he appeared to be just the kind of awesome, awe-inspiring teacher the seminary class needed. I mean, it wasn't even the twenty-first century yet, and already he was using PowerPoint to present his lessons. The kids were enthralled. So one day shortly before Thanksgiving, when my husband asked if I "might be willing to consider the possibility of maybe teaching seminary," I was stunned.

"What's happened to Paul?" I said.

"He's drowning. School is taking more time than he anticipated, and he's working extra hours because his wife still hasn't found a job, so he's decided that he just can't do seminary anymore."

"Okay. I'll do it," I said, with no hesitation. Now it was my husband's turn to be stunned.

I explained that I had known for months that I was supposed to be the seminary teacher, but had never told him because I was afraid that if I did, he would actually give the CES coordinator my name. Besides, I didn't want him to rely on *me* for the inspiration; he was the bishop and needed to receive his own revelation.

"I did receive my own revelation, but I ignored it," he confessed. "I know how you are in the morning, and I honestly didn't think you could handle teaching seminary. But apparently the Lord thinks otherwise."

At my orientation meeting, the CES coordinator assured me that to be a successful seminary teacher, I didn't need to be a scriptorian or an entertainer; I just needed to love the kids. I believed him, but I also believed that I needed one more thing: divine intervention.

Here's how I know that I got it: When I began teaching, our ward was on the 1–4 p.m. Sunday meeting schedule. Six weeks later, we switched to the 9–12 slot. When the alarm jolted me awake at 7 a.m. the first Sunday in January, I thought, *It can't be time to get up! It's too early!* A while later, after the fog cleared, I realized that every school day for the past six weeks, my alarm had been going off at *4:40 a.m.* and I had been getting up. *Immediately. Every morning.* And I had been *lucid.* Obviously, God had been performing this weekday miracle so I could fulfill my seminary responsibilities. On Sundays, however, He was going to leave me to roll out of bed on my own, just to make sure I got the point.

I got it. I taught seminary for three years and never missed a day. Even more miraculously, one day I overheard one of my students say to a friend from another ward, "You don't like seminary? Dude, you should come to *our* class. Our teacher is *awesome!*"

Truly, with God, all things are possible.

RELIEF-ISTAN
E. Victoria Grover

IF RELIEF SOCIETY were a foreign country, which it pretty much has been to me all my life, then I'd say it lies somewhere in the southwest region of the former Soviet Union—an area rich in natural resources, containing many local attractions, but never holding much appeal for me. If I had my choice, I'd spend my time in some other foreign country—say, India. Serving in Young Women's is like visiting India—colorful costumes, ancient rituals, exotic spices and pheromones in the air, and lots of glitter. I love going to India! Or Primary, which feels like a busy rural town on the shore of a tropical sea, somewhere in Central America. It's full of light and laughter, little children everywhere in various states of dress and emotion. I've lived happily in Primary for years and years.

Not that I haven't visited Relief-istan over the forty years of my adult life: I've even spent several months there, off and on. Mostly when I was much younger—in the 1970s and 1980s—newly married, one child born in 1978 and three more on the way, and at the same time finishing my education and starting my career. The natives in Relief-istan usually tried to make me feel welcome, but it seemed hard for them to imagine a place for me within their culture. I was such a strange, foreign, maybe even dangerous creature: a woman who was also a professional—a mother who worked outside the home.

When my husband and I moved into rural northern Maine in 1981, we both had good jobs. Because of a nearby Air Force Base, our ward was very large. Before my first calling in Primary, I attended Relief Society faithfully, and almost every Sunday I listened to lessons admonishing us one way or another that one of the principal evils in the world was the mother who worked outside the home. For many years there was only one other employed woman in our ward, and she was a teacher who walked to and from school with her children every day (as she often reminded us).

My children stayed with a babysitter. Oh, and did I mention that I'm a mediocre cook and the inside of my home looks like an old storage shed? This accurately reflects my interest in cooking and decorating, a secret it didn't take long for the Relief-istanis to figure out.

I've spent my adult Church life going back and forth between teaching in Primary and Young Women's. In between those responsibilities, I attended classes and activities in Relief-istan. I tried to be accommodating to the native culture, but I continued to be myself, just trying like everyone else to become my *best* self. I continued to advance in my professional career. My children grew up and did *not* end up in jail. As the years went by, Relief-istanis came to accept my presence in the ward. Love me or hate me, I simply was not going away.

I was spiritually busy enough; I had plenty of my own stumbling blocks to work on, so I was not in any position to waste much time throwing stones. But other than visiting teaching and a very brief stint in 1992 as a substitute Cultural Relations teacher, I held no Relief Society callings during my thirty-plus years in our ward until five months ago when the bishop asked me into his office and called me to be the new President of Relief-istan.

I have accepted every calling I have ever been given—part of a deal I have with God in my patriarchal blessing—so I automatically accepted this one too. Of course I was shocked, blown away—all those verbs you think of when you're suddenly hit with the reality that "past performance is not a predictor of future results." But it is an understatement to say that *I did not feel good about this calling!* It did not feel even remotely right. It *certainly* did not feel *safe*.

The next Sunday I was sustained in Sacrament meeting and two hours later I walked through the door into Relief-istan. I was already loaded up with assignments from the bishop. I felt confused and disoriented. I took my seat in the chair set up for the Relief Society president, my two counsel-ors, whom I barely knew, sitting on either side of me. I asked my first counselor to conduct the meeting. And for the first time in many, many years I sat in an LDS Church meeting and thought "What the heck am I doing here?"

Stranded like a beached whale. Marooned in a foreign country. A stranger in a strange land. I waited for the natives to start stoking the fire and putting the human-sized kettle on to boil. I watched the faces in that full room, expecting to see the lean and hungry look that would spell my doom . . . but instead they mostly looked . . . well, preoccupied, like most busy women look today. Some of the old timers who'd known me since I first came thirty years ago looked a little nervous. But the newer women, who'd only known me for the last few years or didn't really know me at all, actually smiled at me.

By the end of that meeting I realized this was a much bigger deal to me than to almost anybody else; it was time to get some perspective and some information. I needed to do a lot of reading. Reading and praying—I can't cook, but I can read and pray very effectively. I went home and read the new Church Handbook—twice—and every talk I could find on lds.org given by a member of the Relief Society General Presidency in the last five years. I prayed—very repetitively, I'm afraid, but the Spirit is forgiving. I began to get an idea of what I might be able to do in this calling that would be useful.

During my worst times in the Church, I've said, "This is my Church as much as anybody else's, and nobody is going to drive me out!" At the best of times, with humility, I've seen opportunity in the adversity and suffering that came from being a different kind of Mormon sister. I used the loneliness, rejection, and inevitable misunderstandings to build my own reserves of patience, compassion, empathy, charity, forgiveness, and especially my working knowledge of reconciliation.

In the five months of my administration, our ward Relief Society has been changed by me, and I have been changed by it. Don't get me wrong—I'm still me and I know what it means to run a show, and I am running this show. But I love my Heavenly Parents and my elder brother Jesus Christ, and I'm beginning to love what I'm now called to do in their Church and of course, that means I'm beginning to really love the women I am serving. Experiencing that love is truly partaking of the most rich, sweet, and delightful fruit of the gospel. Who could ask for anything more?

So welcome to Relief-ista . . . I mean, welcome to Relief Society. Bring your worst self and your best self, and join us in the struggle: the work, the fun, the conflict, the love. Just remember, we're all in this together.

All of us.

Every. Single. One.

MY SPIRITUAL APPOINTMENT
E. Wells

WHEN I WAS an undergraduate at BYU, Elder Neal A. Maxwell came to give a devotional address. In his audience of students, there were many people who were or soon would be making important life decisions—about what to study, what career to pursue, and where to live and decisions about marriage and family. Elder Maxwell's message was that, in his view, there were many decisions in our lives about which God would not have specific direction for us—that we should make wise and good decisions, but that for many things God would be equally happy with whatever choice we made.

But, said Elder Maxwell, there would be times in our lives in which God would need each of us specifically to do something that one of us uniquely could do. He called these moments "spiritual appointments."

That idea and that phrase stuck with me over many years. I had callings. I served. I think I did things that sincerely helped people, sometimes doing things anyone could have done, sometimes doing things I was particularly suited to. But it wasn't until many years after hearing that devotional address when I came to what I feel quite sure was a spiritual appointment with God.

I was teaching a Gospel Doctrine class. The course of study that year was the Book of Mormon, and the section I was to teach that week included 2 Nephi 5, in which Nephi describes God as "cursing" the Lamanites with a "skin of blackness" so that they would be "loathsome" instead of being "white," "fair," and "delightsome."

I struggled to figure out how to teach the lesson. The verses are, in my view, completely repugnant. I am not a person of color, so I can only imagine how difficult it is for my brothers and sisters in the gospel who are to read these verses. Of course, one approach would be just to ignore those verses, to teach the lesson about other topics covered in the section. But it seemed to me that doing so would essentially treat the verses as if they were not a big deal, which implies either an implicit acceptance of what those verses say or a denial that what they say is tremendously painful. I was unwilling to do that.

Another approach would be to use the kinds of apologist dodges that I have heard before in Church: "The curse is the denial of the priesthood. The black skin is only the *sign* of the curse." That seems to me to be little better, and there is no support for it in the passage itself. I was unwilling to do that either.

That really left only one choice, which was to take the verses square on.

I am a very experienced teacher, both at Church and in my profession. Teaching and speaking at Church does not ever make me nervous. But as I was preparing to teach this lesson, I was more upset than I have ever been preparing to teach.

The night before the lesson, my husband came in to find me sobbing in the bathroom. I explained to him that I was terrified to teach the lesson. I was terrified that I would say something wrong, that I would offend someone and wound them worse than the language in the text already had. My husband asked why then did I just not teach those verses? The answer was that I felt absolutely spiritually compelled. I felt strongly directed that I had to—however scared I felt—teach the lesson I had prepared.

The next morning, as I prepared to teach, my hands were shaking and I could hardly draw a steady breath. I began my lesson by saying that I had really struggled in preparing the lesson, because the lesson covered a passage in the scriptures that I really hated. I read the verses in question and said that I thought the language used was ugly, that there really wasn't a way to read "loathsome" that was not insulting and offensive to a person of color.

I told the class that in preparing my lesson I had considered both ignoring the passage and offering an apologist interpretation of it and described the reasons I had rejected either approach as legitimate. Then I said that I didn't know why that passage was there, but I explained that I don't think any passage of scripture should be read in isolation because the scriptures are the work of a lot of authors, a lot of translators, and a lot of passage of time.

I argued that our goal should be to find the "red thread" in the scriptures, by which I meant that we should look for the elements that weave through the pattern over and over again, that *that* is what we are meant to find and focus on. Then I read a series of passages from the scriptures reaffirming that God is no respecter of persons, that he invites all to come unto him, and in the words of Nephi himself later in 2 Nephi that God "denieth none that come unto him, black and white, bond and free, male and female; and he remembereth the heathen; and all are alike unto God, both Jew and Gentile." (2 Nephi 26:33)

I asked for other people to comment, not sure what I would get in response. I remember many of the comments, but then came one that I will never forget. A man stood up in the very back row of the class. He said that he had been raised Mormon, but that he had not been to Church since he was a teenager, and that a large part of the reason was because of the very passage that I had focused on in the lesson. He thanked me for giving him a way to understand that verse that did not imply that God thought less of people because of their skin color.

That was the moment that I realized that this had been a spiritual appointment in which God needed me, and me specifically. Years of teaching Gospel Doctrine have given me the "red thread" view of the scriptures, and years of teaching both inside the Church and out made it possible for me to believe that—as much as it frightened me—I might be able to speak honestly and compassionately about such a difficult topic. Because of this, I believe that I was able to say to one of God's sons exactly what he needed to hear on the one day in years he had come to the place where he could hear it.

WORDS HAVE POWER
F. C. Guymon

I HAD SACRIFICED HOME, friends, family, and a great town to live across the country to make a better life for my family. I finally was collecting a few fun friends in our new ward, and the ward split! Boy, was I mad. Boy, was my hubby mad!

We made it a point to have a daily walk at 6:30 a.m., and we walked and used lots of angry words as we walked. Words like, "How could they do that to us? We are the only ones our age who got left behind! We live in a poorer area so we got separated! I can't be Young Women president anymore! We are stuck with the less fun group! We will never see our friends in the same way again!"

Well, you get the picture. We really slathered on the negativity like hot tar. We began to enjoy the heated commonality of our conversation. Every meal for the week began and ended with "ain't it awful!" subjects.

Then, our new bishop ruined it all by asking us both to come to his office together to receive new callings. He was in for an earful. We were fully armed and loaded, and we shot a lot of arrows his way. My spouse was asked to be the Young Men president and I a seminary teacher. I knew right away I could turn that one down because it was an "assignment" (at the time), not a calling, and I did so, very self-righteously. Spouse reluctantly said he would think about his new calling. We both went home rather deflated. What went wrong? We couldn't be feeling guilt, could we?

We knelt down for our prayer together and prayed to understand what to do. All during work the next day, I pondered the conversation with the bishop. I did not realize my husband was doing the same thing. Finally the word "murmur" came to me. Oh my gosh, we had virtually become Laman and Lemuel with our bishop as Lehi!

Paul and I discussed the real possibility of going back to the bishop to ask forgiveness. It was going to be really hard to humble myself and admit. But as my "guilt brakes" are better than the brakes in any top-of-the-line vehicle out there, Paul and I set up appointments with the bishop. My husband went in alone and came away feeling much better. Our bishop had also thought his calling over and felt very strongly that Paul should not be the Young Men president after all. As I ended my conversation with the bishop, I told him I would think about the seminary teacher thing for one more day and call him back. Paul and I came home relieved that we caught ourselves before we damaged our testimonies further. I was very humbled and felt a huge burden lifted.

I had made covenants in the temple that I would help build up the kingdom of God wherever I lived, and I was going to make the best of it no matter the circumstances. So, as I knelt to pray that night, I was unprepared for the huge "bolt of lightning" that went through my whole being as I asked Heavenly Father for an answer as to whether or not I should serve as an early morning seminary teacher. I had never felt such an immediate reaction in my life. There was absolutely no doubt as to what I should do.

I called the bishop the next afternoon and began to share with him my recent experience with prayer. I paused and heard him sniffling.

"What's wrong, Bishop?" I asked. He tearfully answered that as a new bishop, he prayed to the Father that I would know in a very real way that I was supposed to accept this calling, and that I was his first "miracle" as a bishop.

The lesson learned is that murmuring is as addictive as any drug on the market. Words have power.

CLEANED AND SHOWERED
Jeanne Decker Griffiths

THE HOT, TROPICAL city of Bangkok is notorious for its terrible traffic jams. I sat in the car fuming, and the morning rush hour traffic wasn't even that bad.

"Well, it may not be bad traffic yet, but I will be lucky if I can make it back home by late afternoon. Besides, I hate baby showers. I hate all those typical games they play," I grumped.

Being in the Relief Society presidency, I felt obligated to go, but I resented having to give up my whole day when I had other pressing obligations waiting for me.

Just as New York is "the Big Apple," Bangkok, the tropical equivalent, is called "the Big Mango." Our branch with over a dozen different nationalities was the only English-speaking LDS church unit in this teeming city of nine million people. This of course meant our "boundaries" were huge. Bad traffic didn't help. I lived downtown in a high-rise apartment building with my three kids and my husband who worked several blocks away at the US Embassy.

The baby shower was for Leslie. She and Somchai had built a house on the outskirts of town in a residential Thai neighborhood. With the new baby, they now had five kids, plus a pack of dogs to help control the snake population that occasionally infested their yard. At that time, there was no highway to get to their house. More gloom descended as I thought of slogging through all that local traffic. I would probably get home about the same time the kids got back from school, if I was lucky. My irritation spiked.

Then my thoughts turned to Leslie, a sweet American

sister who would probably be in Bangkok for the rest of her life. She had met Somchai, her Thai husband, when he came to the States for graduate school. When they seriously considered marriage, Leslie came to Thailand to meet her future relatives and make sure she knew what she was getting into. Despite the advance preparation, she discovered after the wedding how ill equipped she was to deal with the cultural shock of her newly adopted country. She cried through her first year of marriage and was terribly homesick.

But that all changed when Leslie found the Church. The gospel gave her a spiritual home, and the Church members became her extended family. Thailand seemed a lot less foreign with the loving support of our English-speaking branch. Somchai, a lifetime Buddhist, never joined the Church, but he was always supportive of Leslie's Church activity.

"She stopped crying when she joined the Church," he once explained, "and since then we have been much happier."

As I thought of this, I realized I wasn't going to just any awful baby shower. As a member of Leslie's Church family, I was going to celebrate the birth of a new family addition. This event was a statement of my love and support for a dear sister who would never again live in the United States with her biological family. Even if it wiped out my day, attending the baby shower was the least I could do.

Despite my new resolve, I still felt emotionally immobilized by the resentful feelings that engulfed me. How could I get rid of these negative feelings? I felt incapable of doing it on my own. So while driving through Bangkok traffic, I offered a sincere, heartfelt prayer, humbly asking God to remove all my irritation and resentful feelings so I could give my full support and love to Leslie.

What happened next was quite remarkable. I have never had a prayer answered so quickly and in such a physically dramatic way. I felt a small energy source that started in my chest.

It was like a little spiritual vacuum cleaner, collecting every speck of irritation and anger. But unlike a typical vacuum, nothing was forcefully sucked in. Instead, all my negative feelings willingly allowed themselves to be absorbed. It made me think of Doctrine and Covenants 121:46: "and without compulsory means it shall flow unto thee."

I could feel all those negative, angry feelings gently flowing into that little spiritual vacuum cleaner as it slowly moved up thru my body. Having now collected every resentful, negative particle in my being, I felt the little vacuum cleaner continue to move up through my body, until it exited out of the top of my head. And with the removal of those bad feelings, I now felt a sweet, rich peace envelop me. Along with the peace came an enlarged desire and capacity to love.

I had certainly heard of the transforming power of the Atonement, but I had never experienced anything like this before. I felt incredibly blessed. Not only for the miraculous change of heart, but also that God had allowed me to observe His "house cleaning" methods. It was a glorious feeling knowing that God needed me to make a difference in someone's life and then gave me the resources to do it. I didn't realize He was so willing to extend his love to us as we offer to pass it along to others.

Yes, knowing that I was on God's errand made all the difference in the world. It was the best baby shower I have ever attended. And the games weren't so bad after all.

THE LITURGY OF JELL-O[19]
Kristine Haglund

THERE ISN'T ENOUGH time to discover a thousandth part of our heritage of faith as Mormon women. Yet, I have come to accept that some people—even smart, wonderful people whom I love—just don't want to hear more stories about "pioneer women." And although this sentiment is profoundly alien to me, I can imagine how it might arise.

First is the simple fact that these women's lives can seem so utterly unlike ours that it's hard to figure out how their stories should matter to us—it can be hard to find the connecting threads.

Second, and I think more common, is the problem that we use these stories to measure ourselves by, and usually end up feeling that we fall short. It's easy, with the benefit of hindsight and the record of so many concrete, tangible difficulties our foremothers triumphed over, to be sure that they did enough for their faith. It's so much harder (maybe impossible), from the middle of *our* lives and struggles with forces that are harder to see than drought, crickets, mobs, and diphtheria, to believe that we too might be faithful enough—that the small ways we give our lives away each day, for the gospel's sake, are worthy and excellent sacrifices.

I want to turn our hearts to our mothers. There's a truth they understood, that is perhaps harder for us to grasp. It's in the Section 131 of the Doctrine and Covenants: "all spirit is matter."

For our foremothers, sheer physical survival demanded heroic efforts, and it's easy to see how those efforts contributed to building the kingdom of God. They were, after all, building a literal, physical kingdom in the tops of the mountains. They raised new generations of Saints by birthing them, sometimes in appalling physical conditions, but with much greater assurance that if they could only keep their children alive, they would be doing their part to swell the ranks of the Saints. Housekeeping took on religious significance, as cleaning floors and killing flies, sewing clothes and finding clean water, were all part of the project of civilizing the wilderness. Taming the desert was the collective expression of conquering the natural man and woman.

It is easy to think—as we buckle our hospital-born children into carefully engineered car seats while listening to the radio, setting the GPS, and trying to ignore the cell phone as we drive a pioneer day's journey in half an hour—that it is different for us, that our physical and spiritual lives are separate, and that our challenge is to find time away from our material surroundings to practice our religion. But we would be wrong to think so.

For us, as for our forebears, the ordinary dailiness of our lives is shot through with mystery and holiness—our love of God manifest in our love and care for His creatures and His creation. The rhythms of our spiritual lives are grounded in the same kinds of discipline as our physical lives. Like laundry and dishes, prayer and scripture study and Sabbath observance have to be done over and over again, until they work themselves deep into our bones and into our souls.

There are, perhaps, moments when the impossibility of extricating the spiritual from the physical is apparent: when you wake your teenagers for seminary or family prayer, are you (and they) performing physical or spiritual labor? It's both, of course. You are helping them inscribe the practice of Mormonism in their bodies, even if their minds are still mostly asleep. Likewise, we're promised that the physical observance of the Word of Wisdom will yield not just physical health, but also "wisdom and great treasures of knowledge." When we labor over a healthy and beautiful meal, we know we are nourishing souls as well as bodies.

We can learn from the seamlessness of consciousness that is so appealing to me in the histories of Mormon women. Here, for example, is a series of diary entries from Patty Bartlett Sessions, an early Utah midwife:

> Thursday 4. My birthday. Fifty-two years old Febr 4 1847 in the camp of Isrial Winter Quarters. We . . . drank a toast to each other desireing and wishing the blesings of God to be with us all and that we might live and do all that we came here into this world to do. Eliz Snow came here after me to go to a litle party in the evening. I was glad to see her. Told her it was my birthday and she must bless me. She said if I would go to the party they all would belss me. I then went and put James Bullock wife to bed [i.e. assisted at the beginning of labor] then went to the party. Had a good time singing pray-ing speaking in toungues. Before we brake up I was caled away to sister Morse then to sister Whitney then back to sister Morse Put her to bed 2 o clock.
>
> Friday 5. This morning I have been to see sister Whitney. She is better. I then went to Joanna [Roundy]. She said it was the last time I should see her in this world. She was going to see my children.[20] I sent word by her to them. I then went to the Silver Grey party. Eliza Snow went with us. I danced with Br Knolton Mr Sessions not being well. Joanna died this evening.
>
> Saturday 6. Made soap. Visited some that were sick then went put sister Whitney to bed. She had a son born eleven o clock P M. . . .
>
> Sunday 15 [14] Went to meeting then in the evening col-lected Zina Jacobs, Eliza Snow, sister Marcum [Markham] at sister Buels to pray for Sylvia and child that they might be delivered from bondage and Windsor and David come here with them. We prayed sung in toungues spoke in tongues and had a good time. Then went put Sister Oakley to bed. Child born 4 oclock A M.
>
> Monday 15. I have been out all night had no sleep. Visited the sick all day.

Tuesday 16. We wash. Visited the sick. Sister Young died at sister Holmons.

Tuesday 23. Visited the sick yesterday I cooked for the widow orphan and poor that they might feast and have thier hearts made glad today in the counsel house. . . .

Monday 15. Put sister Stilman to bed. Visited the sick. Sister E R Snow came here last night. She has done me up a cap and wrote me some poetry which she composed which I shall write here. [There follows the poem, "Composed for Mrs Patty Sessions By Miss E. R. Snow March 15 1847," the first stanza of which reads:]

Truth and holiness and love,
Wisdom honor, joy and peace—
That which cometh from above,
In your pathway shall increase.[21]

The activities are strange to us, but we recognize the pattern: the mundane and miraculous, the holy and homely tumbled and swirling around and over and through each other, in the eternal round of a consecrated life. We fulfill the sacred duties as we participate in the small daily work of belonging to Relief Society. We perform the liturgy of Jell-O, prepare the sacramental postpartum casserole, supply the oil of tenderness and the grace of a listening ear. From the very beginning, Relief Society has been about sewing shirts *and* being endowed with power from on high; the grand and glorious work of preparing ourselves and the world for Christ's return is performed not usually in grand gestures, but in the daily work of writing God's love into our own bodies and inscribing it on the fleshy tables of each other's hearts.

And how could it be otherwise? We love and serve a God who made Himself known to us in the particularity of an ordinary human body, who sweetly washed His disciples' feet (and what is more weirdly and awkwardly human than *feet*?), and whose body was anointed both before and after He performed His saving sacrifice by women, who were His most constant disciples and friends.

OUT TO LUNCH . . .
AND DINNER THEATER
Lael Littke

IWAS OUT TO lunch when they distributed administrative skills. So several years ago when I was called to be second counselor in Young Women and put in charge of raising money for girls camp, I despaired. My pleas of being a square peg fell on deaf ears.

After a dismal thought-trip through the Land of Can't, I changed direction. I looked at what I'd been successful at. During the '70s and '80s, I'd been the writer part of a dynamite roadshow team, a jolly group of grasshoppers who regarded singing and dancing as the way to give the large number of kids in our ward a fun, positive experience.

Okay, so we'd do a show. And dinner. But time was short, and we had only seven active Young Women then. I presented my idea to them. They were enthusiastic. "A Mystery Dinner," they requested. Good.

I let them design the characters. They lined up OoLaLa LaFitte, a French maid; Bonnie Clyde, a gangster's girlfriend; Beulah Bankbuster, richest woman in the world; Bambi Pompon, cheerleader; Twiggy Two, model; Desdemona MacBeth, Shakespearean actress; Tootsie Toodles, ballerina.

Now the script. Not wanting to deal with murder, I wrote "Who Spilled Uncle Will?" The seven cousins, above, have been called to Uncle Will's mansion for the reading of the will after his death. He has been cremated. The urn containing his ashes is discovered on the floor, empty. Who spilled him, and why? Each character has reason to have done it.

The plot was complex; the time short. We had an actor in our ward who did amazing voices. I enlisted him to narrate the play, providing all the different voices as the girls acted it out. His wife was wardrobe mistress of our local playhouse. She put together colorful costumes.

The evening was a resounding success. I learned a lot about leadership. First, desperation is a major ingredient. Second, think of your strengths, not your weaknesses. Third, you're not in it alone; every ward has talented people to help. Fourth, if you carry a clipboard and look official, people will follow you. Fifth, if you combine food with a measure of creativity, a group of lively young people, and a lot of prayer, you end up with really fine memories for all.

SHELTER, SAUCE, AND SERVICE
Mendy Waits

FOUR YEARS AGO, I found myself organizing a dinner and community service event during the slushy days of a Pittsburgh Spring. My partner in crime (aka, the second counselor in the Relief Society) and I had three weeks to get it together.

Let me be clear about a few things. I don't like to speak in front of groups, or prepare dinner for sixty people, or cold call businesses asking for donations, or ask people to donate food and time. Also, there are some women I really don't like working with. I had to remind myself many times that serving in the Church has never been about what I like to do. I obviously needed a lot of help.

We showed up at the chapel that Thursday evening, three hours before Go Time. Our crew: four women, three toddlers, and an infant in a carrier. We set up round tables first, then chairs. The bags and donations were sorted and organized, ready for the crowd that would come to assemble them. Husbands dropped off food and picked up children, and we forced a mandatory rest on our seventy-two-year-old Relief Society president. Then we started dinner preparations.

As the women trickled in, filling the chairs and filling the air with voices, I hurried the Gorgonzola cream sauce for the pork loin. I nearly scorched it, but I was saved by the newest arrival (a graduate student) willing to watch it simmer while I introduced our guest speaker from the Women's Shelter. I welcomed everyone to our commemoration of the founding of the Relief Society. While I looked at the familiar faces, four women moved silently in and out of the kitchen, bringing plated dinners on huge trays, as I recounted the early history of our group. The night progressed with relatively few hiccups and, naturally, ended with cake.

I was happy to announce to our sisters the following Sunday that the director of the shelter had contacted me to let us know our contribution was the largest donation the shelter had ever received. I basked in their satisfaction. I so often like to keep myself on the periphery, but it felt good to give in to that feeling of sisterhood.

My story is not unique. Scenes like this play out all the time in LDS chapels around the country and around the world. This is the power of the women of the Church. With limited funds, short notice, and only our rag-tag talents as resources, LDS women mobilize for funerals, weddings, humanitarian aid, or whatever is needed. We don't always like what we have to do, and we don't always like each other, but let it be known that we GET IT DONE.

OUR SISTER ANN
Sheila Duran

IN THE 1980s, close on the heels of the battle over the Equal Rights Amendment, Ann Stone was called as the Relief Society President by a new, young bishop, just into his thirties. She was a single LDS mom, whose nonmember husband had suddenly succumbed to a brain aneurism at forty-two, leaving her to raise two young boys.

The bishop was forward-thinking enough to include Ann in every weekly priesthood executive council (PEC) meeting, instead of asking her to just attend the monthly ward council meeting. He valued her observations and insights, realizing that perhaps the "all male" factor of the PEC would miss something important in discussing the affairs of the ward and its members, more than seventy-five percent of whom were women and children.

Ann was responsible for at least two legacy projects that still resonate all these years later. First, she suggested that as a congregation we could start volunteering at a local homeless shelter by preparing and serving the evening meal one night a month. She proposed that the different auxiliaries and quorums would rotate; Relief Society, Elder's Quorum, the High Priest Group, Primary, Young Men, and Young Women organizations would each take two evenings a year. The resistance came from the oddest of places. The High Priest Group leader was quite reluctant and wanted to know if the ward funds were going to pay for the food. He thought that their wives could do the cooking.

Ann held her ground, maintaining that the contributions from the member groups would be an opportunity, and that the organization members themselves should do the preparation. There was a lot of harrumphing, but other High Priest group members got wind of it and made it their challenge to find recipes and develop their skills. One fellow was a particularly spectacular hot-roll baker and others followed suit. It is a long-running outreach into the community for the normally insular LDS community.

One unintended consequence of this is that when one of Ann's now-grown sons formed a men's book group, patterned after the one his mother founded thirty years before, the guys all agreed that they—not their wives—would be responsible for the refreshments.

The second legacy was Ann's desire to help people coming from the Intermountain West to the prairies of Illinois to feel a connection to the very state that held rich pioneer history. The Relief Society room was decorated by an original oil painting of the High Uintah Mountains of Utah, commissioned in the 1960s by the stake Relief Society presidency. It was there to honor—and serve as a reminder of—many members' emotional and spiritual home. We had a wonderful woman in the ward (from Utah), Jean Hinckley, who was an accomplished nineteenth-century-style quilter. She had taught many of us how to piece and quilt by hand.

Ann asked Jean to design a quilt for the Relief Society room wall that spoke of our prairie pioneer heritage and celebrated the good qualities of the Midwest. Multitudes of women from the two wards participated by contributing nine patches that formed part of the Amish Friendship Circle design. The colors chosen were all prairie colors. It took two years to complete; it hangs there still and provides a warming, welcoming touch in our meeting space.

Ann passed away in 2006, but her influence and insight still inspire us.

AND HE GAVE SOME, PASTORS
Kristine Haglund

Ionce had a bishop whom I loved, and who loved me. I thought I was very special to him, but I have since learned that most of my friends in the ward thought they were particularly beloved as well.

Once, the day after my visiting teacher and I had talked about Alma 5, about receiving Christ's image in your countenance, I happened to see the bishop across the street at a distance of a couple of hundred yards. Unbidden, but also undramatically, came the thought "Oh, that's what it looks like."

There was nothing spectacular I could point to, no special light emanating from his face, no transformation of his physical features (indeed, the best description I've ever heard of his physical aspect was from a friend speaking in sacrament meeting, who said that the bishop looked like a very large and exceptionally distinguished auto mechanic. It seems about right, and he laughed heartily, so I think it's okay to repeat it). He just looked kind, and that kindness somehow overwhelmed every other impression one might have had.

Later on, a decade or so after I had moved away from his ward, I was desperately seeking inspiration about what was (and remains) the most difficult, soul-tearing decision I have ever had to make. I was (and remain) lousy at distinguishing impressions of the Spirit from the restless, neurotic activity of my imagination, so I went to the temple fasting and praying fervently that if there were words I needed to hear, that there would be someone there at the temple to say them to me in a way I could hear and recognize.

It turned out to be a good thing I hadn't been hoping to receive vivid inspiration on my own, because I spent the whole session near tears after walking in and seeing my dear old bishop for the first time in years, and sitting next to his wife (whom I also adore). Neither of them walked up to me and said, "the answer to your question is," but they both listened to me lay out the problem, and said something completely unexpected, which freed me from the agony of the questions enough to make a decision possible. My bishop is still a young man, but he has had a series of major illnesses in the last few years, each seemingly crueler than the last. The first life-threatening crisis happened in November a few years ago, coincidentally a few months after I had gotten divorced. He spent days in the ICU, then several more days in the hospital, before being discharged just a couple of days before Thanksgiving. The next morning, early, he called my ex-husband, whom he barely knew, and said "I'm so sorry for the belated invitation—I'm hoping you might be able to join us for Thanksgiving dinner."

He knew I had family close and would be okay, but remembered, miraculously, that my ex-husband did not, and he wanted to make sure he wouldn't be alone. This thoughtful gesture was both astonishing and unsurprising, typical of my bishop's way of ministering. The circle of his love is always expanding, not because he casts his net wide (though he does), but because he loves individuals so deeply that his caring inevitably overflows to those around the ones he first cares for.

Last week, I heard that he was in the hospital again, after

another serious crisis of a new and unexpected kind. I was furious. Every time I went to pray for him, I ended up sobbing in frustration, livid like a petulant child at a god who would let such a good man suffer so. I know better, and I should have more faith. But I don't, and so I raged and sent petty blasphemies heavenward at regular intervals for a few days.

And then one day, out for a morning run, I passed their house, just as the door opened. And there he was, walking slowly and a little too carefully, taking out the trash. I managed not to cry right in front of him, but I wanted to, out of pure joy at seeing his kind face. We spoke briefly, and I spent the rest of the morning repenting, vowing to learn to patiently take out the trash instead of demanding that the universe be ordered as I deem just.

I wonder if our heavenly homecoming will be a little less grand than we dream, less like the triumphal march of returning heroes, and a little more like my clumsy encounter with one of God's best servants in the driveway the other morning. Perhaps He will look up from his work, and embrace us, even though we are grubby and a little stinky from the labor of getting there—and then we'll both go back to our work, and it will seem just a little easier and more joyful, lightened by the grace of our belonging.

TAKING CREDIT
Susan Young

WHEN I WAS twenty-five, graduated from BYU, and working in Provo, I was called to serve as the education counselor in the stake Relief Society of the BYU stake I had attended for three years. At the time I accepted this calling, I would describe myself as naive, intense, devoted, and highly spiritual. I believed that I had been called for a specific reason, and I prayed to know what I might do to serve the sisters of our stake, half of whom were young married women (students and the spouses of students, many with small babies) and half of whom were single (students or other young working women like myself).

Their needs varied widely. Where the single sisters were concerned about classes and grades and finding someone to marry, the married sisters were working on relationships with their husbands and patience and self-control in dealing with their children. What program of education could I propose for the Relief Society that would be meaningful to all the sisters? I fasted and prayed to know what the Lord wanted for them, and my answer was that I should try to help them come to know the Savior better, to achieve a close personal relationship with Him.

This was the worthiest of goals, but I had no idea of how to achieve it until I read in the year's leadership materials that the General Relief Society Presidency had challenged all the sisters to read J. Reuben Clark's *Our Lord of the Gospels*, a compilation of all the scriptures of the four New Testament Gospels grouped by incident and arranged in chronological order. This book was essentially a biography of Jesus, a coherent story of His life, from His premortal identity as described by John ("In the beginning was the Word, and the Word was with God, and the Word was God"), to the announcement of the angel Gabriel to Mary that she would be the mother of the Messiah, to the Resurrection of Christ after His death. I knew that this was my answer: I should focus my efforts on getting the sisters to read this book because it would help them walk with Christ through His mortal life and give them a sense of His presence in their own lives, of His closeness and willingness to laugh with them, suffer with them, and strengthen them in overcoming their own trials.

With the complete support of the stake Relief Society president, my ward education counselors and I did many things that year to encourage our sisters to read *Our Lord of the Gospels*. We divided the book into weekly assignments that required no more than about ten minutes' reading a few days in each week. We had sisters occasionally report in weekly Relief Society meetings on something they had read that increased their testimonies. We mimeographed (this was before the era of the copy machine) each weekly reading assignment because sisters who couldn't afford to buy the book could simply take the list of scriptures and look them up in their own Bibles.

At the end of the year, I planned to sponsor a fireside that would bring all the sisters of the stake together (and brothers too, if they wanted to attend) to hear a talk about the Savior from someone whose testimony was powerful and who could convey that testimony to others.

It was this fireside that complicated my altogether positive, faithful sense of my calling. I don't remember who suggested that I ask Brother Jeffrey Holland to be our speaker (a friend in law school? One of the ward education counselors? A roommate?), but I contacted him by calling his secretary, and he agreed to speak. This was before his appointment as the president of Brigham Young University and long before his calling as an Apostle. He was a professor, and he was known for his testimony of the Savior and as a respected as a leader. I scheduled the Provo Tabernacle for the Sunday evening of the fireside.

I, of course, had proposed these plans in our Relief Society presidency meeting and received the enthusiastic support of my sisters. The stake Relief Society president sent me to the next stake council meeting to have the stake presidency approve of our plans. We both thought of the fireside as no different from all the other meetings and events we had sponsored, a routine request that would be quickly approved. At the meeting, I made my two-minute presentation, after which the stake president said, "Yes, that will be fine," without discussion. The next day I started to work on the posters and flyers and contacted each ward education counselor about announcing the fireside in the next week's sacrament meeting as well as Relief Society.

Then, less than a week before the fireside was scheduled, I got a call from the stake Relief Society president. She told me that the stake president had contacted her to say that it was inappropriate for the Relief Society to sponsor a fireside. I was stunned, to say the least, and immediately angry about two things: first, that he hadn't called me when I was the person he had been dealing with, and he knew that I was in charge of the fireside; and second, that he didn't raise his concerns—if he had them—in the stake council meeting when I presented our plan.

His actions seemed insulting to me on both counts, an assumption that he could ignore me, pretend I was of no consequence, and obliterate an event that was very important in the bringing together of the work we had done in strengthening the testimonies of the sisters of the stake. It did not even occur to me to question his claim that the Relief Society should not sponsor firesides, but when I talked the matter over with a friend, he said, "Any freshman or sophomore club on campus can sponsor a fireside; a mere group of friends can hold a fireside." My friend was right, which made the stake president's reason for intervening in our plans even more questionable.

I knew the scripture in Doctrine and Covenants 42:88: "And if thy brother offend thee, thou shalt take him between him and thee alone," so I called up the stake president and asked to meet with him. "I don't feel good about this at all," I said. "I've already invited Brother Holland to speak."

"The stake presidency has decided to sponsor the fireside," he said, "so that you won't have to embarrass yourself."

"Embarrass myself? Why would I be embarrassed?" I asked.

"Having to tell Brother Holland that you've overstepped your bounds." He declined to meet with me, saying, "We'll handle it. There's nothing else that should concern you," before he hung up.

So there was to be no discussion in which I could explain how hurt I was, no explanation of why the stake president felt he should take over our plans, no reconciliation and coming together in concern and love. I was accused and shunted to one side. The stake presidency would take up any further contact with Brother Holland.

How did I respond to this situation? I just continued with the final preparations for the fireside, ordering the refreshments and reminding the education counselors to ask ward members and especially the sisters to attend. I didn't try to get the stake Relief Society president to protest the stake president's actions, or resign from my calling in protest, or call up Brother Holland to tell him why I wouldn't be the one greeting him Sunday evening. I didn't defend myself, my inspiration or my work. As I try to understand why I continued to play the role I had been given, I think it is because I had been treated similarly on enough occasions that I just accepted such behaviors from empowered men.

And even though I was so upset, I kept in mind the inspiration I had received about our Heavenly Father's desire to increase the testimonies of the sisters in our stake. I fasted and asked the Lord to comfort me and to prepare everyone—men and women alike—who came to the fireside to be touched by the Spirit and to receive a personal witness of the Savior's love.

Which is exactly what happened. Elder Holland spoke of Christ's Atonement as one who had studied and prayed diligently to be able to understand its immense significance. The meeting was deeply spiritual. I don't know how many lives were changed, but many, many brothers and sisters told me that Elder Holland's testimony communicated to their very souls. It was confirmed to me that the Lord's greatest desire is that we should turn our hearts to Him, and that Christ loved me as well as all of the members of our stake.

It is evidence of what a searing, formative experience this was in my life that it is still on my mind forty years later. Much older and more experienced, I am not at all naive about the possibility that priesthood leaders might act in ways that are neither inspired nor in accordance with Christ's gospel. I've learned that sooner or later everyone will have reason to be offended by a Church leader, and that each individual needs a personal testimony of Christ and of the truth of the Church in order to thrive despite such injury.

I hope that if I were in such a situation again, I would stay focused on the work Christ had given me, forgive the stake president, accept his human frailty, and keep in mind the goodness in the hearts of my fellow members of the Church. But I would want to do these things as someone who does not agree to her own mistreatment, even as she would not agree to the mistreatment of someone else, but as someone who realizes her value and the value of the work she has done for the Lord. In other words, I hope I would make the same choices but act from a position of truth and strength rather than as someone who has been injured and silenced.

MISSIONARIES AND MARSHMALLOW SHEEP
Steffani Raff

I WOKE UP UNAWARE of where I was. The familiar sensation of needles jabbing my feet and calves woke with me. I had fallen asleep kneeling beside my chair, again. I rubbed my legs and looked at the clock. I had been in a kneeling position for just under an hour now. I closed my eyes and restarted my prayer. I began with an apology for falling asleep, but before I could finish my penitent thoughts, the words started to slur and I was slumbering—again. It didn't matter what time I prayed, day or night it was the same. I was simply unable to stay awake for my personal prayers.

My fourth baby was irritable and generally didn't sleep longer than an hour at a time during the first eighteen months of his life. I was up and down consoling this unhappy baby so much, I felt like a shell of my former self. Inside that shell, feelings of unworthiness crept in and made residence. What kind of person was I if I couldn't even say a full prayer?

It was Sunday and I was rushing my four children out the door and into the car. We were running late—again. I knew my Primary lesson was on Ammon and missionary work, but I hadn't had the energy to prepare anything to keep my very active class of seven- and eight-year-olds engaged. I hadn't even had the energy to read the lesson—just the title.

I prayed as I buckled children into car seats. "I'm sorry I was too tired to prepare a lesson this week, and I don't feel like

I deserve any help here, but I love these children. Please give me an idea of what to do with them."

Two thoughts came to my mind: marshmallow sheep and the ward newsletter. I grabbed a bag of marshmallows. The children in my class would love acting out the story of Ammon, especially if it meant protecting marshmallow sheep.

I had no ideas about how to use the ward newsletter, but I picked it up and drove to Church. During sacrament meeting I opened the newsletter to one of the missionary letters in the back. Taylor Roderick was serving in Greece; I skimmed his letter and tears came. He was discouraged because they could not find anyone to teach. They had done everything they could to find anyone who might listen to their message but with no success.

I opened my Primary manual, the objective of the lesson was: "Heavenly Father watches over his missionaries." In my mind, the ideas came and I knew what I needed to do.

During class, the story of Ammon came to life as each child took a turn protecting King Lamoni's marshmallow sheep. As the well-guarded "sheep" were eaten, I shared Elder Roderick's letter with the children and invited them to share ideas of what they could do to help one of Heavenly Father's missionaries. They decided to draw pictures of Ammon to send to Elder Roderick and to pray for him that Heavenly Father would help them find people to teach. The children prayed for him for weeks; I know because several parents reported to me of their child's very specific prayers for Elder Roderick.

A few months later I shared another letter with my Primary class; Elder Roderick reported finding "some great college students" to teach and another investigator who was giving up coffee and smoking. He wrote, "We're grateful to have found them. I'm sure that we've had some extra help from everyone's prayers. Especially the younger voices. They seem to lift higher than ours do. (Thanks to Steffani's Primary class.)"

"Did you know your prayers could make such a difference? I asked them. The sweetness of the Spirit testifying Heavenly Father heard and answered their prayers filled the room.

I sat in awe. This kind of experience only happens to really great members of the Church who have everything together, or at the very least who don't continually fall asleep while they are praying, right? Heavenly Father reached beyond my "tired" in that moment to teach me: He loves me. My efforts are enough.

THE "BONDING COMMITTEE"
Meghan Busse

MY HUSBAND AND I served for several years as the head of the Activities Committee in our ward. When we started out, the committee felt a bit beleaguered. It felt like the Put-up-the-chairs-and-mop-the-floor-one-more-time Committee. We started to have the committee meetings in our home. We spent the first few minutes socializing, and sharing what we thought the highlights of the last activity had been, making sure that we noted anything we had learned to improve the activity the following year. Then after the business of the meeting, we served dessert. We invited people to bring their spouses and their kids to the meeting.

This had two important effects. 1) The people on the committee felt appreciated and valued for the good work they had done and 2) The people on the committee began to be friends.

This had tremendous effects. First, people who are friends with each other throw much better parties than people who don't know each other or don't feel they have anything in common. Second, the Activities Committee still *did* have to put up the chairs and mop the floor, but that is much more enjoyable if you are doing it with friends after you've just put on a successful activity that people appreciate. The consequence was that we did put on better events that were more fun, and better accomplished the goal of helping people in the ward make personal connections with each other.

But we also did this within the committee itself. The Activities Committee became a place in which people who didn't quite fit in could quickly feel that they did fit in, and made a valuable contribution. Activities Committees as such don't exist in the church these days, but plenty of other committees certainly do. The principles we learned can be applied to a variety of situations.

WRESTLING WITH THE GOSPEL
Kelly Austin

A TYPICAL SUNDAY TEACHING the seven-year-old class went something like this: two or three boys would be wrestling in a back corner of the classroom, grunting and shoving their way through the hour; two other children would be sitting in their chairs, poking at one another, seemingly tuned out to the lesson itself, especially with the commotion in the back; and two little girls would sit on the edge of their chairs, ready to bombard me with serious gospel questions.

Clearly, each week was a struggle to figure out how to address each of these different personalities. One Sunday, frustrated with the apparent inattention of the class, I asked one distracted child to repeat what we had just discussed. Without hesitation, he recapped the entire lesson. When he finished, he said, "but I was thinking . . ." and added his own observations on the Book of Mormon story we'd been studying.

I was stunned. Another boy even piped up and added some additional thoughts. Apparently, something was sinking in after all. From then on, the wrestling and the nonsense seemed less insidious. After all, if they could tune it out, so could I.

Then there were the two girls eager for Gospel instruction, always ready with a new question. These weren't the ordinary questions of a seven-year-old. They were, instead, questions like "Why does God let Satan tempt us?" or "How did God become God?" or "If my mom doesn't make it to the celestial kingdom, can I still visit her?"

Obviously, the CTR manual didn't cover these topics. But, judging from their eager faces, I also knew they expected real answers, not just the "Primary answers." Of course, I couldn't really prepare for their questions about the nature of eternity or the apparent injustice of mortality. But they certainly motivated me to study more, to pray more, and to seek the Spirit more.

As I think back on teaching this class, I am reminded of the scriptural account of Jacob's wrestle with the messenger of God. I watched these children wrestle with the gospel—both physically and intellectually. And their questions caused me to wrestle with my knowledge and understanding. I suppose that's what Church stewardship is all about: growing and stretching and refining. Sometimes it's painful; often it's noisy and messy. But for the most part, the struggle is worth it.

MY MENTOR, MARCELLE
Marilyn S. Beatse

I JOINED THE CHURCH in 1956, as a sophomore at Brigham Young University. I had agreed to attend BYU at the urging of my "inactive" father who clearly knew that once I was there, I would enjoy myself and become a Mormon. His hope that I would marry a "good Mormon boy" came true in 1958. In 1962, my husband graduated from college, and we moved to Southern California with our young son and soon-to-be-born daughter.

Marcelle Jones was the West Covina Ward Relief Society President. She approached me at Church the first Sunday we attended, and my life changed forever. She took me under her wing, taught me how to be a wife, how to be a mother, and how to serve others. My own mother had died when I was sixteen. Although I had learned to care for my father and brothers at a young age, I had not learned the concept of service beyond my own family.

Marcelle continually asked for my help in serving others. Her guidance and support pushed me to talk to people I had never met and do things I had never done. She taught me how to organize and plan meals for large groups of people—including feeding women for three days at a local Education Week. She taught me that decorating for an event or setting a lovely table is an act of service and a way to honor the women in Relief Society. She always said, "Make the sisters glad that they came to Relief Society."

I was called as a Relief Society counselor to Marcelle a few years after I met her. Along with other women from our stake, we drove to Salt Lake City for the General Relief Society conference the year the song "As I Have Loved You" was introduced. I will never forget singing that lovely song all the way home from Salt Lake City.

Marcelle was the guiding influence in my life of service, and the embodiment of that song. Her guidance and incredible example of service taught me that taking a meal to someone else isn't a burden; it's a gift. She taught me that service to others didn't have to be fancy; service needed to just be given in love. I have served in the church for fifty-five years now using all the skills taught to me by my leader, friend and Relief Society sister, Marcelle.

STAYING POWER FROM MY CHILDLESS FRIEND
Sherrie L. M. Gavin

I "QUIT" THE RELIEF Society a few years ago. The term "quit" is a lie; one cannot quit an organization from which they are assigned based on acceptance of Church membership, gender, and age. But I found it too difficult to attend.

"This is your role in life!" said an acquaintance in Relief Society. "Your job is to serve women who are mothers." Her words sounded as though she were assigning me slavery. I was unable to have children so I must serve those who did? I preferred to stop attending than to keep hearing this kind of skewed thinking.

Once in a great while I would stretch my head into Relief Society. One such occasion was at a Relief Society Christmas party. The theme of the party was a celebration of the General Relief Society presidents. The Relief Society education counselor had assigned women to read short biographies and quotes from these Relief Society leaders. Toward the end of the presentation, she explained that she wanted to include something about the (then) freshly assigned General Relief Society president, Julie Beck. As Sister Beck was new, the resource used for the party was absent of information on her. "But," the counselor explained, "Sister Beck is a mother of three children, so she can relate to all of us, only as mothers can."

I left the party long before dessert was served. In the weeks following, I tried to strike the whole thing from my mind. After painful years of fertility treatments and failed adoption applications, I felt branded as worthless and unwanted. I questioned if I could remain in a Church atmosphere that seemed to mock my personal limitations, but the thought left me almost as soon as it came. To leave the Church seemed to deny Christ, and I could not live without friendship of the Holy Ghost.

At some point, it occurred to me that Eliza Roxcy Snow was not quoted in that Christmas program. The time allotment had not allowed for a quote from every member of the General Relief Society presidency, and Eliza wasn't included. I had long loved Eliza's work, insomuch that I could only think of her as a friend, by name. How could they not quote Eliza? I sought consolation and reprieve in her poetic words, but found myself drawn to biographical information about her. In this, I had a grand revelation: Eliza didn't have children!

Tears intermittently flowed as I feasted on everything Eliza. She was beautiful. She was educated, a writer and a "poetess." She added extra fabric to her dresses so her feminine skirts would best shape her womanly frame. Child-bearing did not define her, yet her words had mothered me at times when I could not find empathy or companionship elsewhere.

As I read of Eliza and her words, I was not alone. She was there, mothering me, teaching me, one childless woman to another. She not only survived crossing the plains while protecting the records of the Relief Society, she thrived and nourished the re-establishment of the Relief Society into season. She understood the barren, and she understood the fruitful. She was defined by her service to Christ. The miracle borne to me that Christmas was one of understanding: Relief Society is an organization for women who are dedicated to Christ. And like Eliza, I will not quit.

My work as a family therapist and my Church experiences lead me to believe that although "unrighteous dominion" is less common in the Church, it is often even more painful in that setting because our wards and stakes are supposed to be safe places. — Debra Blakely

---

LIFTING THE HANDS
THAT HANG DOWN
Connie Susa

EVERYONE KNOWS THAT members of The Church of Jesus Christ of Latter-day Saints give of themselves. They provide compassionate service of food, child care and transportation. They forgive one another their trespasses, and help others move in or out of their ward. Add that to their official callings to visit families assigned to them, teach weekly or monthly lessons, head an auxiliary or the ward library, expand public relations with the community at large, etc., and Latter-day Saints are a busy lot.

That is why, when members go beyond Church service to support civic affairs or to care regularly for an aged neighbor, they are maintaining a charitable lifestyle that overflows the wide brim of their proffered cup. These are the celestial beings who broadcast love wherever they go, and our family has been the blessed recipient of many of these saints.

In spite of our son's multiple disabilities and his specialized technology, Mark has attained middle age in the heart of our community. I took him to Cub Scouts until his troop found it constraining to camp within his limits. When Mark had no opportunities to go out with friends, my husband John ensured that he had stimulating activities in the community every weekend.

Having retired last year and losing his vision, however, John cannot continue to provide for all Mark's activities. While we love Mark as much as ever, we both see our roles shrinking as we age. Thus, John sought out PLAN, an award-winning program that provides personal support networks for vulnerable people in Canada. With the help of like-minded parents, he learned the details of the model and replicated it where we live in Rhode Island (PLAN RI).

Members of Mark's network have come from many sectors: a road running partner, a woman who worked for the bus company where Mark served an internship, former students of John's graduate class in special education, people in the human service field and relatives. All share some interest with Mark, including the newest member who is an avid cyclist and willing to train with Mark on his low-slung CAT Trike.

By far, however, most members of Mark's informal

supporter system share the common thread of Church membership. One of the earliest, certified as a special educator, testified in our due process hearing that from her observations in Primary and elsewhere Mark would be able to handle the distractions of a typical classroom. Jennifer helped open the door to his inclusive and normalizing education, and brought him a gift bag of school supplies before his memorable first day in a typical sixth grade.

Faith, a lifelong friend from Church, socialized with Mark, taking in movies and lunch periodically. Then when she was conducting a fund-raiser, Faith gave Mark the opportunity to contribute at the Rock-a-thon. Some sponsored him, but Willie went further to staff a rocking chair next to Mark and keep him company for part of that long afternoon.

Pamela invited Mark to cook and enjoy dinner with her family, in spite of the extra effort it takes to help him up their stairs. In response to our other son Frank's fight with Hodgkins' Lymphoma, Pamela sponsored a walking team at the Leukemia and Lymphoma Society fundraiser. Mark was an integral part of that team, proud to be fighting the disease that had threatened his brother.

Among the newest members of Mark's personal support network is an LDS professor of geography at Rhode Island College. Seth welcomed Mark as an auditing student in his classes. Every week, Mark came home from class raving about some exotic region or distant city. And once a month, his family carries out a fun activity with Mark. Who could have imagined Mark pedaling his fluorescent orange CAT Trike and Seth wheeling in Mark's orange wheelchair around the half-mile circle in our neighborhood? Like all the efforts of Mark's committed brothers and sisters, that ride emanated a bright glow throughout our neighborhood.

Carol and Walter have family in New York City, so when they were going to spend the weekend there, they provided transportation for Mark to enjoy a weekend with his big brother in Manhattan. The two bonded as adults, separate from their parents, while John and I enjoyed one of a few respite weekends in thirty-five years of parenting.

We especially cherished the large family from Church who lived right in our neighborhood. Mark was close enough to wheel over spontaneously and watch the progress as they laid a new patio. He read to their younger children and showed them the intricacies of his wheelchair. He offered more advice than any of them needed, about the care of an older brother's broken bone. Before they moved out of state, the family used Mark's uniqueness as a way to educate their children about diversity and the desirability of looking beyond the obvious differences.

On the other hand, nearly every member of Mark's network has given him advice in the mysteries of negotiating the social scene, one even bringing a teen-aged daughter to help explain the perspective of a young stranger whom Mark had frightened. And when Mark's penchant for late bedtimes threatened his equilibrium, members of the network learned about the technology that would help track Mark's sleep and signed up to phone in bedtime reminders every week. Those calls, too, help them bond further with Mark.

Most learned in a network meeting where Mark's seventy-two-hour kit is kept in his apartment. While no one person has been designated to support Mark through a natural disaster, no one would turn down a call for help from the vulnerable man they have befriended.

Chris has taken Mark all the way to Colorado to visit his family and brought his band to play at one of Mark's annual backyard cookouts. One young mother has figured out how to fit quality time in with Mark. She plans to bring her two active toddlers to Mark's for an hour or so of coloring. Her husband is a medical resident, so she will help Mark understand various body functions as they color in the pages of his simplified Gray's Anatomy coloring book.

Brothers and sisters in the spirit, each member of Mark's network has committed to be their brother's keeper in one way or another. They have each contributed to the abundance in his life and to the assurance that he will continue to enjoy meaningful relationships in the future. They have provided a serenity of spirit for John and me as we face our transition beyond the veil. They live the admonition of Peter:

> And above all things have fervent charity among yourselves: for charity shall cover the multitude of sins. Use hospitality one to another without grudging. As every man hath received the gift, even so minister the same one to another, as good stewards of the manifold grace of God. (1 Peter 4:8–10)

"NO" LESSONS
Diantha Nebeker

M Y FRIEND MARTHA, our Relief Society president, recently did something that astonished both the men and the women in our ward simply by saying "no" at an appropriate time and place.

The stake patriarch had been invited to give a Friday evening fireside in our ward, which had been duly announced in Sacrament Meeting several weeks in advance. The Sunday before this event, the bishop surprised Martha by announcing in ward council that there would be a dinner before the fireside provided by the Relief Society. Martha somehow managed to retain her composure and not leap across the desk and rip the bishop's throat out.

Instead, she calmly told the bishop that Relief Society would not in fact be able to provide dinner on such short notice, reminding him that the sisters were already in charge of the Munch and Mingle that week, and there wasn't time to organize both. By all accounts, the assembled brethren were more than a bit startled by this response, but Martha stood her ground.

In the end, the High Priests agreed to organize the dinner, and they actually did it themselves, having apparently gotten the message from Martha that it would not be wise to pass this responsibility along to their wives. (And no, Martha hasn't been released from her calling.)

Men in leadership positions can learn that it's not a good idea to make assumptions about the women they are supposed to be serving without asking the women what they actually want or would be willing to do. But they will most likely only learn this if women have the confidence to set them straight when their assumptions are incorrect. Sometimes serving in the Church means saying what you mean and standing by what you say.

President Barbara Winder, eleventh Relief Society General President, said that, when working with priesthood leaders, "[Women] are invited to come with solutions. Together [we] can talk about ideas to see what will work. The priesthood brethren expect and need the perspective of the women in the Church. We need to be prepared to assist them."[22]

RELIEF SOCIETY BEGINNINGS
Kate Holbrook

WOMEN ALL OVER the country in 1842 created benevolent societies. They would get together and ask "how can we make things better for this world?" Then they would form a society and write by-laws for their society.

Sarah Kimball, an early Mormon woman, did this, too. She got together with another woman who didn't have a lot of money and they thought, "Let's start a sewing society, and we can sew clothing for the men building the Nauvoo temple." They had a meeting and they thought through what they wanted to do. Eliza R. Snow wasn't at the meeting, but she was known as a woman of letters, so they asked her, "Will you be our secretary, and will you write up some by-laws for us?"

She did, and she took them to Joseph Smith.

Instead of having the sisters rest with the sewing society, he made them part of the Kingdom of God. He organized them the way the Church was organized. He said to them, "I now turn the key to you in the name of God, and this Society shall rejoice, and knowledge and intelligence shall flow down from this time."[23] A sewing society was a great idea. It would have accomplished a lot of good, but this—The Relief Society—was better.

This was more. This was eternal and tremendous.

THE BISHOP'S WIFE
B. Garff

T HE BISHOP'S WIFE calling is not an official calling nor does it get a direct sustaining vote. However as the Bishop's Wife I felt very much sustained. Our loving and watchful ward family cared for us in many ways: hugs and treats; dinners for new Bishop's Wife babies; ward members, young and old, to provide extra hands during busy sacrament services; supportive notes or glances that said, "We support you . . . both of you . . . all of you." Often, the sustenance came from sympathetic souls who listened to the stress that comes with the Bishop's Wife calling while at the same time never speaking ill of the Bishop because of his lack of presence at home. That balanced sympathy felt really good.

I was certainly not a very matronly "Mother of the Ward," and I learned how very human the wife with the Bishop's Wife calling is. I had many baby gifts I wanted to give that never made it into the wrapping paper; and many meals my heart wanted to make, but my "mother of young children and Bishop's Wife" self said not to run faster than I had strength.

At home, and especially on Sundays, I found myself setting my expectations at "Realistic" instead of "Idealistic." We would come home from Church, usually to a house that looked like it had been ransacked by robbers, and strip off our Church clothes to jump into our comfortable ones. After a quick snack of nachos or cheese and crackers, my children would ask to watch a "Sunday show" (which usually turned into hours of Sunday Shows). "Sure," I replied, while I would then revel in the quiet while I cleaned up the chaos and . . . gasp! . . . often took a nap. The rest from that nap would go a long way toward more patience on those interminable Sundays.

As we partnered as Bishop and Bishop's Wife, I fortunately did not feel envious of the spotlight, nor was I pushed aside by the calling. The Bishop, through his words and actions and struggle for work and life and Church balance, let us know that family came first in his heart despite the demands of the calling.

Of course, there were many times when my side of the partnership felt heavy and my imperfections were uncomfortably glaring. We were usually late to Church, and I often had the loudest kids that made the biggest mess. Some mornings before Church were just plain rough. Maybe the kids were unruly. Maybe I was feeling especially inadequate. Maybe I just couldn't handle walking in to church twenty minutes late and feeling like everyone—which, I emphasize, was really no one—was judging the Bishop's Wife because she was late again.

With tears of "I can't do this job" in my eyes, we would quickly break off to the Primary room to listen to sacrament meeting, and I would try to hide those tears if someone happened upon us. After days like that, precious priesthood blessings, available at anytime, would reassure me of God's acceptance of my service and His complete understanding of all that I was doing and feeling. Those blessings proved to be the Balm of Gilead.

The Bishop and the Bishop's Wife together grew up a lot. We became more understanding and less judgmental. We learned not be hurt by misjudgment. We learned to serve more as we were privy to and in awe of the many quiet acts of service rendered, and we knew that these were just the tip of the service iceberg.

Most of all, the Bishop and the Bishop's Wife learned to love more those we serve and to feel greater love for our

Church leaders. Bishops privately and endlessly plead for individuals in their wards. The members' heartaches are the bishops' heartaches, and their joys are also his joys. The Bishop's Wife indirectly pleads for the "anonymous-to-her" individuals by pleading for the Bishop's heartaches and worries. And, because we know of this private pleading, we can imagine how our other leaders are pleading for and loving us.

In all of this, the Bishop and the Bishop's Wife are reminded that all of this is about the Savior's love and His ultimate pleading for us.

WHEN IT RAINS . . .
Alyson Beytien

IN AUGUST OF 2011, our area received fifteen inches of rain in twelve hours. The flooding was massive and devastating. The visiting teaching and home teaching calling trees began, and the list of flooded basements and homes began to grow.

I was a counselor in our Relief Society, and received the first call from a family who lived twenty minutes outside of town. The lower level of their home—which included garage, laundry room, bedrooms for five boys, food storage, tools, family heirlooms and two cars—had been underwater for eight hours. The mother took her kids to her sister, then headed home to start the cleanup. She was uncertain exactly what she would need, but knew that they needed to get everything out in the air and start to clean. We arranged for eight to nine ward members, including my own family, to head out to their home that afternoon.

The ensuing months of cleanup, repairs, remodeling, and

reorganizing that came to numerous families in our ward highlighted the good, the bad and the ugly of giving service in the real world of true disaster. Our Relief Society president asked me to be the "point" person for this particular family and coordinate the clean-up, repair, donations, and all other service that needed to assist the family. I became privy to the polar ends of service; unknowing, selfless acts and selfish, arrogant demands.

Initially, numerous ward members offered furniture, bedding, clothing, and other necessities needed for the family. They had lost every piece of clothing they had for their five boys, and all the beds, furniture, toys, books, and paraphernalia that come with children. School was to start in one week so all their school supplies were unusable. I kept an Excel spreadsheet of available items, who had what, when it would be available, and what was needed. I kept lists of money donated for the purpose of supporting the family.

The first two weeks of the disaster had amazing instances of selfless service. A sister drove to the family's home every day to take their laundry, clean it that night, and drive it out the next day for the exchange. A couple showed up at the house with pizza and soda for everyone when dozens of ward members were cleaning out the mud and slop. There was constant care of their children in other member's homes. The family lived in the basement of another ward member for two weeks while the water and electricity was turned off. The numerous acts of service were inspiring, and reaffirmed our ward's commitment to each other.

But the cleanup and repair dragged on. Our city and area were not declared national disasters, so funds were not available to provide for all the damage done. There began to be contentions among the members about what work should be done for the family, and what work was "over the top." I had phone calls from members who had offered to donate furniture, who did not want it donated to Family A; only to Family B. There was gossip and derision of the Relief Society presidency by many who felt that either there had been too much service given, or not enough. Or not the right kind of service.

Coordination of donations became difficult as some ward members talked to the family directly and offered money or goods and then an identical item or amount was brought to the family from the "list" which was accepted also. Some ward members felt that the family was taking advantage of the situation to acquire "top of the line" appliances, goods and a remodeled home.

As I attempted to navigate the miasma of spiritual, emotional and temporal needs, I couldn't help but wonder what would happen if we truly had an epic disaster. After the initial surge of compassion and support, pettiness and selfishness reared its ugly head. I was appalled, frustrated, and stunned at the change in the attitudes of many as time dragged on. I was also amazed, grateful and stunned at those who maintained their Christlike demeanor and consistently answered the call to help.

The real test of service comes from maintaining our Christlike charity even when we disagree with the "how, where or when" of charity. Our ward members did not know the full situation of the family; and they shouldn't. Financial, emotional, and spiritual status is something that the Bishop, Relief Society president, and Priesthood leaders should know. That knowledge informs the amount and direction that service takes. Service is not a democratic decision.

GROWLING AT GOD
Louise Plummer

Several years ago I was standing in my kitchen on a Sunday afternoon, minding my own business, when I got a phone call from a member of the stake presidency asking me if I could come and visit with him in an hour at the stake center. I said "Oh sure," my voice musical and pleasant as Snow White. But after I hung up, a deeper, more disturbing voice came up: "What could he possibly want?" I asked my husband.

"He's probably going to call you to a job," Tom said.

"A *stake* job? I don't want a *stake* job." I stamped my foot like a troll. "I'm done with *stake* jobs. They're useless. Stakes are useless. I want to work at a grassroots ward level. Stake people have meetings that no one wants to attend. Stake people visit wards whose members cringe when they see you. I don't want a stake job. I don't want it. I won't do it."

"Then say no," Tom said, escaping into the living room.

"I will," I shouted. "I'm not doing it. No one can make me!"

Silence, except for the beating of my diabolical heart.

Later, in my car, I ranted at God aloud. "I know I should be grateful for everything, but I don't feel grateful. I'm mad. I know my life is good, but it's not exactly free, is it? I hate the pressure that we're supposed to say yes to everything, whether we like it or not. And say it with a smile. I hate it. There are plenty of jobs for everyone to go around. Why not call on some organized chick for the stake job? Call on someone who likes to boss people around. You know I hate this kind of stuff.

Why are you picking on me? I'd rather be hit with a bolt of lightening than take on a stake job."

At the stake offices, I sat in the waiting room fuming grimly. I wanted to be angry with the stake president's counselor, but he was much too charming a man, greeting me warmly with a smile and a handshake. I stopped grimacing and sat down with him in his office.

He said, "We've asked Deanne Francis to be the stake Relief Society president, and she has asked that you be one of her counselors."

Without a beat, I said, "Oh, I'd love to work with Deanne. That will be fun. Yes, I'd be happy to."

So what happened? Well, Deanne Francis happened. She was someone I had only a nodding acquaintance with, but I enjoyed running into her on the odd occasion. I knew she was married, had a family, and that she was a practicing nurse. I knew she was in the same high school class as Tom, and that she had been head cheerleader some thirty-five years before. I knew she was smart and likable.

I mean, why not? Who cares if it's a stake job?

On the way home in my car, I apologized to God, again aloud: "Okay, I'm sorry I was so crabby about the stake thing. It's going to be great. I really like Deanne. I'm sorry. I get afraid. It was the fear speaking. Thank you. Thank you. Thank you."

Soon after, we sat together on the stand in stake conference, along with Janet, the other counselor, and were sustained. Deanne handed me a couple of manuals. One had a light blue cover with the word "Homemaking" in the title. My mouth dropped. "I'm the homemaking counselor?" I whispered to Deanne. "Me?"

She smiled broadly and said, "You'll be fine."

"I'm the homemaking counselor," I told Tom after the meeting.

"I'll loan you my recipes," he said.

And so came my first fall leadership meeting—that meeting that I thought no one wanted to attend—but in fact all wards were represented. I had called ward counselors ahead of time to ask what kind of help they could use, and everyone said the same thing: ideas for homemaking meeting. I assigned them to show and tell the best activity or craft they had recently had in their individual wards. Meanwhile, I went through my files of "things I might want to make some day," and among other things found a pattern for a five-inch stuffed calico bear that made a fine tree or mantle decoration for Christmas.

I bought a pert red-and-white calico, cut out some bears, and since I have a combative relationship with my sewing machine, sewed the bears by hand, leaving a hole for stuffing.

I had not bought stuffing. I had no quilt batting. No old pillows to raid for stuffing, no foam pellets.

And then I thought of the one Halloween costume I made for my youngest son, Sam, years before: a tiger costume. I had the same dilemma with the tail as I had with the bears. It needed stuffing and I had no stuffing.

I had toilet paper then, and I had toilet paper now.

I stuffed each bear with wadded toilet paper and finished sewing them.

The meeting went smoothly. Each ward counselor had brought something to share and they were all different from each other. Then I showed my bears. They liked them. They liked my bears. "Very cute," they said. They passed them around. I gave them patterns. "So cute," they said. "So soft."

"What did you stuff them with?" someone asked.

I didn't want to reveal that. For thirty minutes, I had been an excellent stake homemaking counselor and now this nosy question.

"Huh?" I said.

"What did you stuff them with?"

I looked at them sitting benignly in a half circle in front of me, these sisters, who sewed and made elegant decoupage boxes and sweet-smelling gift soaps in the shape of seashells.

"Toilet paper," I said. "I used toilet paper."

They blinked at me as a unit, straining to understand. The giggling began like small birds chirping. Some covered their mouths with their hands, but they all giggled.

I shrugged, sheepish. "Don't get them wet," I said. I told them about Sam's tiger costume and how it had rained on Halloween night and how the tiger's tail had flattened into a mosquito's tail.

Violent, but completely accepting, giggling.

I lived through the toilet paper, the women's conferences, the tied quilts for the Deseret Industries charity, the making of lunches for missionaries, the leadership meetings with my new best friends, refreshments for the Church-wide Relief Society broadcasts, and speaking at ward conferences.

Was it—was I—perfect? *Don't be stupid.* I have dips of growling at God. I give you a final example: one stake conference landed on Father's Day and I was in charge of arranging the flowers. We had a budget so this was a matter of ordering and collecting two large bouquets for the Provo tabernacle. Usually, Tom helped me get them into and out of the car, but on this particular Sunday, he was sick and so were our four boys.

Frankly, I felt that it was a conspiracy of maladies. I grumbled as I hauled the flowers into the car, picturing the five males in my family jumping out of bed the minute they heard the garage door close to play video games. I grumbled in my car: why do I have to be the only one to go to stake conference? I hate stake conference. I struggled with the flowers. I broke into a sweat. I grumbled as I found my seat on the stand. I was earlier than anyone else.

Unlike Job, I cursed God: You want too much. It's never

enough. Picky, picky, picky. I don't care about the celestial kingdom. I don't want to be a busy bee. When is it ever enough? Why can't we hire our clergy and be done with it?

And then the thought hit me that I might be like Korihor in the Book of Mormon, and I grew anxious. I pulled out my scriptures and turned to Alma 30 and read about Korihor. No, I wasn't an anti-Christ.

People gathered into the chapel, the stand filled up and a choir began singing the prelude music. The congregation hushed to listen. I melted a little. "What do you want from me?" I asked God silently.

My mind immediately filled with the answer: love Tom.

That's it? That's what you want from me?

Love Tom.

I melted completely. It was the best stake conference I ever attended. Music, talks—all inspiring. I was glad I was in that stake job, otherwise I would have missed that meeting entirely, that balm of the Spirit, that message from God to love my husband, who I already loved, but I knew I could love better.

THE NORM, NOT THE EXCEPTION
Tania Rands Lyon

WHEN MY MISSION President called me to train a new missionary companion only two months into my mission, I felt terrified. I was green as a shamrock myself—and now I would carry the primary responsibility of communicating in Russian and finding our way around our area on a vast network of buses, trams, and metro lines? Near the end of the day when he had broken this news, I approached him to ask for a blessing to help me shore me up for this frightening new assignment. And that's when my wonderful, patient, wise Mission President did something unexpected.

He allowed a fleeting look of impatience to cross his face and gently challenged my request. Was I sure I needed a blessing for this assignment? I was taken aback. Wasn't it a good thing to ask for a blessing? Wasn't it my right? I explained my fears, and he graciously acquiesced and gave me a blessing of comfort that encouraged me, but his hesitation also taught me something. Taking on challenging assignments is just something we DO as Latter-day Saints. I did have the right to a blessing, but my request was born of fear and self-doubt. Over the years of service in the Church I have come to see the challenge of leadership to be more the norm than the exception.

FROM POTATOES TO WORLD PEACE
Rebekah Neuner

MY MOTHER ALWAYS felt hers was a supporting role. The tenth of thirteen children who grew up on a small potato farm in Idaho, she never had her own box of French fries until she was married. With sisters who excelled in such things as singing, public speaking, and administration, she decided that her talents weren't the type society valued. My mother is kind, empathetic, generous, and a hard and fast worker. In fact I still don't know anyone who can get as much done in a short amount of time as she can.

Throughout my mother's adult life both she and my father have served in their local wards. My dad, an Ivy League trained attorney, always had the "big" callings or positions, whereas my mom served behind the scenes.

Two years ago my father took a Church position of some prestige and soon he and my mother's bags were packed. They were on their way to Moscow, Russia. My mom had never worked outside the home but had devoted her life to her children and grandchildren. Now that we were all married and lived far away, she was struggling to find purpose in her life and hoped to find it in this new adventure she and my dad were undertaking.

Well, she found it. Their first Sunday at the Moscow Mormon congregation she was asked to serve as the Relief Society president. She was soon spending hours each day visiting and serving the women who lived in the large area their ward covered. But she wanted to meet other people and not just those at Church. She started going to events hosted by the International Women's Club (IWC) and soon became friends with women from all over the world, from Honduras to Poland.

At first my mother was intimidated by the education and professional accomplishments of these polished women; they, however, weren't fooled by my mother's humble beginnings and lack of "worldly" accomplishments. These were women who valued character, and they recognized my mom as a genuinely good person who had a strong desire to bless the world.

The IWC is primarily a charitable organization, and my mom was soon involved in projects for orphanages and pediatric hospitals in Moscow. Naturally she used the resources of the Mormon Church and specifically the Relief Society to gather dozens of homemade blankets, hats, scarves, and hygiene packages for donation. People were amazed at what my mom could pull together in such a short amount of time and with such ease. Of course, those of us who know Mom best aren't at all surprised—we know that her lifetime of quiet service in the Church, in our family, and in our small hometown have been ample preparation for her moment in the spotlight.

Word soon spread among the IWC that "there is nothing [my mom] can't do." After being in Moscow for a little over a year my mother found herself as the chief organizer of one of the IWC's biggest fundraisers and *the* social event of the year in Moscow.

Now when I call my mom and ask her how her day was she talks about having lunch at such-and-such embassy with the wife of such-and-such ambassador or meeting with US colonels at the ministry of defense to talk about their donation to the IWC.

I hang up the phone after talking with my mother realizing that you never know how you might make a difference. The important thing is to stay true to who you are and your natural abilities. God values strengths of all kinds and you never know when and where it will be your time to shine.

GOOD WARDS, BAD WARDS
Suzanne Midori Hanna

S O, HOW IS your ward? Is it a good one?"
So often, when we move from ward to ward, conversations with family and friends within the Church touch on what I will call "ward culture." What makes a good ward "good"? I have lived in some wards that others considered "not

very good" and other wards in which members looked down upon those other wards. It has always been troubling to me.

My mother described people in her youth treating her family as though they lived "across the tracks." When I was in high school, I remember a girl moving into our ward who had lived "across the river." I was asked to befriend her. She was shy. I would try to engage her in conversation, but nothing really clicked. Did I do enough? Could we have been friends? Why didn't she respond to me?

When I was living in wards that others would speak about in condescending terms, I felt defensive and protective of those who lived under the cloud of knowing how others in our stake thought of them. In fact, when I arrived in a new city and prepared to buy a home close to my work, the stake president's wife said to me, "uh . . . that's not a very good ward. You might be better off in another ward."

Unbeknownst to me, the bishop of "that ward" had been praying for people to move into the ward because it had been depleted of leadership over fifteen years of boundary changes. The stake president's wife had no idea that she might be undermining the growth of that ward. I wondered, "If that ward is 'bad,' how will it change if everyone avoids it? Is this the way we bear one another's burdens?"

"We know they look down on poor people," the Relief Society president said of those in other, more affluent wards. "We just do the best we can and know that the Lord knows our hearts." Since I had already heard the stake president's wife demonstrate this judgment, I couldn't argue the point. The more I heard disparaging remarks about this ward, the more determined I became to move in.

It was a soul-saving experience for me. I held many positions in that ward and consider those wise and loving members as some of my best friends. One woman was converted to the Church after she had a dream about her deceased parents.

She happened to work with our Relief Society president who was able to help her understand the meaning of her dream. In another case, a man joined the Church through young adult activities, went to Mexico on a mission, and served in our bishopric.

With some years behind me now, I think that judgments placed on certain wards are largely about the person's own relative comfort in crossing cultural lines. If we find people in a ward who help us feel like we belong, that's a "good ward." If we don't find that, and if we depend heavily on others for our sense of belonging, the ward is a "bad ward." In the case of the stake president's wife, I believe she was feeling protective of me because young members of the ward felt lonely there and blamed the ward for their loneliness. She was trying to help me avoid that same fate.

I later learned that her ward also felt depleted of leadership because various members had moved further out to the suburbs into larger homes. Some of those members confided that it would have helped their morale had I moved into their ward at that time. I began to see that these wards became so preoccupied with their perceived lack of leadership that they became competitive with each other.

Perhaps there is another reason for "bad wards." When we become so task-oriented that we can only see people as potential placeholders on the whiteboard of ward organization, something has clearly gone wrong. There may be an ugly cycle here that comes from pressures for numbers, with no regard to ward history, community context, or awareness of cultural divides between presiding leaderships and the local leaders on the frontline. Someone gets a computer printout, looks at the disparity of numbers, and makes a judgment. Weary local leaders often have no opportunity to share the tender mercies and small miracles that form the spiritual and miraculous fabric of a "bad ward."

The younger we are spiritually, the more dependent we are upon others to help us feel attached. No one wants to be lonely, and we can't help being who we are. On the other hand, no one should be criticized for being unable to provide for each person's unique emotional needs when newcomers arrive and want cultural similarity.

The task isn't easy, but it remains: "Feed my lambs."

PRIMARY PROFESSOR
Elizabeth Howe

A S A UNIVERSITY professor for fifteen years, I had become accustomed to cooperation and respect from the students in my classes. Then I was called to teach the ten-year-olds in Sunday school which I think was the Lord's practical joke on me. This was His way of teaching me that I was not the hot stuff as a teacher that I had—let's be honest here—perhaps considered myself to be. Ten-year-olds don't care about your degrees or your awards or your publications.

"Cooperative" and "respectful" are not generally the first adjectives that come to mind in describing children of ten. Nevertheless, I thought I was prepared for them. I had taken the teacher training course; I knew how to use pictures and other visual aids, how to involve them in activities, and how to ask questions that required them to apply the concepts to their own lives. I was, yes, a Master Teacher. I could certainly deal with eight ten-year-olds for fifty minutes a week.

Or so I thought as I watched the students come into our small classroom that first Sunday. I saw immediately that there is a chasm between boys and girls at that age. The three girls sat on one side of the room, the five boys on the other, the girls demure and well-behaved in their lacy dresses, the boys tipping their folding chairs against the wall and balancing on the back legs. The girls paid attention, answered the questions, actually seemed to be learning. The boys talked to each other, pushed, and punched, all the while tilting their metal chairs against the wall, a precarious stance likely to send them toppling one way or another. I learned that I would do all right with the girls, but I needed to get the boys to settle and balance—both in a physical and a spiritual sense—or I wouldn't be able to reach them.

How could I engage these rowdy boys and at the same time keep the attention of the girls? I had long believed in the power of stories—deep, meaningful stories that had happened to real people. For example I could teach them about faith with the story of Mary Goble Pay, a girl just their age when she finally arrived in the Salt Lake Valley in December of 1856 with her feet frozen. The next morning Brigham Young came with a doctor who cut off her toes with a saw and a butcher knife. The boys loved hearing about that, and I had their attention for the rest of the story: Mary's feet became infected, but she wouldn't let the doctor amputate them because Brother Brigham had promised her that her feet would be saved. "A little old woman" she didn't know felt inspired to come and ask her what was wrong, and then came each morning to apply a poultice to Mary's feet and change the bandages until they were healed.

I sought out stories in General Conference addresses, in the *Ensign* and *New Era*, in Church history books. And if I was well-prepared, I felt that I could get the boys to listen as well as the girls. I also made a rule that we all had to keep both feet on the ground and couldn't tip our chairs.

Let's call the one student who kept tipping his chair "Mark," the bishop's son. He was smart, charismatic, and rebellious—a sort of contemporary Alma the Younger. He seemed always outside the class circle, poised at the door or looking out the window. He distracted anyone who sat by him with plans to carry out some mischief or other—sneaking out to Maverik instead of going to Sacrament Meeting or spilling water all over the cultural hall.

After a few months I had learned a great deal about my other students (Tim was a truly gifted runner and loved to skateboard; Megan L. wanted to work for NASA when she grew up; Chris lived for motorcycles; Megan C. was already interested in boys), but Mark wouldn't look me in the eye and told me almost nothing about himself. In a lesson during which I noted the admirable qualities in each student (I had spoken with their mothers), I talked about Mark's intelligence, his skills with math and science, his potential to be a leader. But where most of the students responded with surprise and happiness after this lesson, Mark did not warm to me or behave any better. I couldn't reach him.

I finally decided to ask the bishop to come to our class and sit with his son. I was not, I must say, operating from the best of motives; I was exasperated with Mark and didn't think that he should keep all the other students from learning. I told the bishop I thought his presence would improve Mark's behavior immediately and that the threat of having his father come to later lessons would go a long way toward keeping Mark in line.

Bishop Furr (we'll call him) did not answer me immediately. I was shocked to see that he looked confused and frightened.

"I'm not sure that would help," he finally said.

"What do you recommend?" I asked.

I had only seen the bishop's competence; he had a strong testimony and the leadership skills to run a very successful ward. Now I was seeing his personal pain, coming to realize that he struggled as well to make a connection with his son.

For whatever reason, they were estranged from each other.

I have been around enough to know that there are many reasons for such disconnections, and that they usually involve well-meaning people who are unable to give each other what each needs. I felt the long, ongoing care of this father, his fear that something would push his son in the next few years into the kinds of rebellious actions that have long-lasting consequences. Maybe embarrassing Mark by having his father come to class wouldn't help him.

I realized that the bishop needed my help as Mark's teacher—and the help of every other teacher or leader who worked with him—to keep trying to connect to him. To care for him as if he were my child. To share the bishop's love and anxiety for his son. To help him through his long, complex and often painful mortal journey. I learned that I needed to go back into that class week after week and do my best to get through to this boy.

I tried humor. I tried lightening up. I kept asking Mark what he wanted the class to be like, how he wanted it to proceed. He once said something like, "I want to talk and lean back in my chair because that's who I am." We reached a truce of sorts; nobody could sit by Mark so that he wouldn't distract them, and I wouldn't focus my attention on him but on the other students. We got along, but I don't think I made much of a difference in his life.

I wish this story had a happier ending. Our ward was divided. I followed the growing up of the kids who joined me in the new ward (most of them are married now, the young men all returned missionaries), but after the wards separated, I didn't hear much about Mark until his father's death from cancer a few years ago. Bishop Furr died in his early fifties, and we all worried about what his widow would do to fill such a great hole in her life, as her seven children had all left home. Someone told me that right after the funeral she went to Salt

Lake City and spent several months with Mark, trying to get close to him, to help him stay off drugs and find some direction in his life.

Mark, I guess, has remained the outsider, the kid no one can reach, the child to teach us, in our sorrow for him, to feel Christ's infinite love for the one sheep who has strayed outside the fold. To teach us to hope that because of Christ's infinite atonement, some day Mark will come back.

BEING NOTICED
E. S. Young

LOOKING DOWN AT her shoes, her chin quivering, a student finishes her conversation with the professor before class. I haven't really noticed her before (or anyone else, for that matter) in this crowded classroom in my East Coast university. I recoil slightly from the "tornado" coming my way as she chooses the tablet-armed chair next to me, putting her head down and sobbing loudly. At first I ignore her like the other students are doing, thinking she just needs a minute to get a hold of herself.

The professor watches her take her seat, and then turns his attention to the computer. His kind eyes turn into a scowl, and he swears softly. He eventually gets the antique computer projector to work and begins his lecture, talking over her sobbing as if nothing is happening.

I ask God if I should help. At first the answer is "No." But as her wails grow louder and her sniffling noisier, I ask God again. This time the answer is "Yes. NOW." I touch her arm and whisper, "Are you OK?"

Shoulders shaking, she whispers back, "No."

I realize that this isn't the time for an extended whispered conversation in the middle of class, but I can't just leave it at that. I pass her a note. "Anything anyone can do?"

"Not really," she writes.

"Hang in there," I write back. With a slight surge of panic, I wonder what in the world I can do about this.

After awhile, she stops sobbing, tosses back her hair from her blotchy face, borrows a piece of paper from the student in front of her, and begins to listen and take notes.

Immediately as the professor finishes his lecture at the end of class, she jumps up and charges out of the room before I have a chance to say anything further. Whew. I'm off the hook for the moment. I say a quick prayer for her, knowing that's about all I can do right now.

In future weeks, she'll walk in and casually scan the room until she locates me, then look away nonchalantly as if she wasn't really looking for me. She meets my eyes but never returns my smile. It seems that it's enough for her just to know I'm still there.

I'm amazed to realize that I didn't really do anything about this situation, whatever it is. Sometimes it helps just to listen, to notice.

Based on decibel level alone, this obviously hurting student appears very different from other people I try to look for: the silently hurting, largely invisible women around the edges of Church. Years ago I made a decision to "watch the edges," making a conscious effort to reach out to those who are often easy to overlook. And while this student's loud wails bear little outward resemblance to the unshed tears of women "around the edges," I think many women long to be seen, to be noticed.

Honestly, I think many women who position themselves squarely in the middle of the action at Church long to be heard as well. Whether that longing manifests in noisy tears or silent, unwept tears, my answer is often the same. Most often I don't know what to do about their situations—but sometimes it helps just to be heard, to be noticed.

CHRISTMAS COMFORT IN THE TROPICS
Jeanne Decker Griffiths

YOU WANT US to do WHAT for Christmas?!" I bellowed heatedly.

I couldn't help my irritation from rising. Of course that's not the expected response to your priesthood leader. My sharp tone must have seemed especially out of place here in Thailand. Known as "the Land of Smiles," being outspoken or confrontational is pretty much a cultural taboo.

Since I was the stake music chair, I'm sure President Kasin, a counselor in the Bangkok Stake presidency, assumed this would be a routine calling, so he was shaken by my confrontational tone. What could be so upsetting about being asked to be in charge of a stake holiday program?

Well, let me give a little background. It had a simple beginning when the Bangkok English-speaking branch used "Journey to Bethlehem" for its annual branch Christmas party. At Church, the audience "journeys" in small groups from room to room meeting the angels, shepherds, wise men, and the baby Jesus. This was a delightful way to tell the Christmas story.

Because it was an innovative and fun way to share Christianity in this Buddhist nation, over the years it morphed into a huge public relations event. It had a festive atmosphere with caroling, food, period costumes, and even a replica of an old city wall. Inside the Church building, all the halls and classrooms had been transformed to look like old Bethlehem.

Not everyone was happy with the tremendous amount of work involved, but it certainly made for a magical evening. As it got more complex, so grew the numbers. The last year had 3,000 visitors during the two night event.

Then our chapel, the only workable location for the event, closed for an eighteen-month renovation. With no way to put on "the Journey," what would replace it? I found out when President Kasin called my husband and me to be in charge of "a stake Christmas pageant!"—with seven weeks notice. Seven weeks? Are you kidding? I needed seven months!

Despite being upset, I now felt guilty about my outburst. I apologized to President Kasin and with great reluctance accepted the calling.

But that didn't stop me from complaining as soon as I got home. I continued ranting for the rest of the week as we frantically brainstormed to come up with a new concept that could work in two languages, with our limited time and resources, in this logistically difficult city. Discovering there was no stake directory didn't help.

At the end of that stressful, angry week, something quite amazing happened. Out of the blue, I received an unexpected message from Heavenly Father. The experience completely changed my outlook and removed my anger. It happened on Saturday, during my daily scripture study time. As I picked up my scriptures, they randomly opened to Isaiah 41. The first verse jumped out at me. It read, "Comfort ye, comfort ye my people, saith the Lord." The scripture had a deep effect on me.

I immediately recognized the scripture. Sung by a tenor soloist, Isaiah 41:1 is the opening line of the most performed oratorio in the world, Handel's Messiah. As I read the scripture,

"Comfort ye, comfort ye," I received my personal message from God. It came as a strong, clear feeling that said, "Don't be upset. Feel the comfort and strength that is freely offered by Christ your Savior. He alone is the source of all peace."

I immediately felt comforted and calmed. Gone was the anger that had held me hostage through the week. And with that calming influence, I was now able to put things in their proper perspective. I had been thinking about thousands of potential visitors, instead of remembering the Savior, the true reason for the greatest of all celebrations. And with that new feeling of comfort, I now felt reassured that everything would all work out. Amazingly it did.

First, my husband—a former missionary to Thailand—wrote a cute Christmas skit in Thai. We prayed for help and fortunately found a mother and her nine-year-old daughter who agreed to enact the drama. They even did so with the requisite humor.

I organized a stake choir, a more difficult endeavor to do in Thailand than in the States. I needed to find some interesting musical arrangements that were still appropriate for their skill level, and then dressed up the music with the few available instruments. It took some work to get the music translated and dispersed in a city of nine million. With the huge distances and Bangkok's terrible traffic, it was logistically difficult to have one big stake rehearsal, so I did a lot of running around on Sundays meeting with smaller groups. Lastly we found someone willing to put together a slide show. With stake assistance we rented a huge screen, performance platform, and sound system.

The big day arrived. Depend on the Thais to know how to have a good time. After a dinner with lots of great Thai food, the program followed with a cute Christmas story, a stake choir, and a slide show. It wasn't "Journey to Bethlehem" with the required help of hundreds. And with no advertising, 3,000 people (fortunately) did not attend. It was a new concept that thankfully turned out well.

For me the real significance of the event was receiving a personal message from God, and feeling His accompanying love. Now when I occasionally feel overwhelmed or stressed, I think of Isaiah 41:1 and remember the time God willingly offered his support and spoke comfort to my soul.

HELPING A SUNBEAM
Z. Huntington

I CAME TO PICK up my son from his first Primary activity in the Cultural Hall, a Valentine's Day party, where they decorated sugar cookies and wrote valentines for missionaries and some of the lonely people in our ward.

As I chatted with the Primary president, Lonnie, we stopped, hearing a man yelling at a kid down the hall, the kind of yelling where you think, "Three more seconds, then I'm going to have to say something." This was the type of discipline that shouldn't happen in one's home, much less in the Church.

But then I heard the crying and froze. That was my son crying.

The man rounded the corner into the Cultural Hall, yanking my crying three-year old by the arm, continuing to yell at him, and then he saw me.

"Your kid is OUT OF CONTROL! HE SHOVED MY DAUGHTER BECAUSE HE WAS RUNNING AROUND THE CHURCH!" He jerked my son's arm, covered in pink frosting, toward me.

"J, I'm so sorry," I said dumbfounded as I tried to calmly

take Daniel's hand. "I need to go clean him up. Lonnie, could you please handle this?"

I don't know what I expected Lonnie to do. Did I think she would talk to him as the Primary president? Did I think he would listen to her because he had a business relationship with her husband? I'm not sure. All I knew is that I had to get my kid away from that man quickly.

I overheard Lonnie while I cleaned up Daniel in the kitchen adjacent to our Cultural Hall. Well, I didn't hear her words, but I heard her tone. Clear, firm, conveying shock and dismay.

Several moms and Primary teachers were there while Lonnie talked to him. They all came up to me afterward, saying how proud they were proud of her. She was talking to a man who was clearly out of control and had a reputation for discounting women and their opinions. She said things like, "J, I don't care what he did. What *you* did is unacceptable, and you did it in the Church."

What happened in that hallway is up for debate, too. Daniel was too young to get an accurate picture, and it upset him whenever we tried to talk to him about it. Other Primary kids witnessed the event, but each day, the story got worse as the kids talked about the event with each other.

The event doesn't matter. What happened was wrong and hard on everyone.

I like to focus instead on what happened afterwards. Those women who witnessed J dragging Daniel into the Cultural Hall made it a point to take care of Daniel. Lonnie didn't stop with lecturing J. She talked with the bishop. She made sure that he understood how damaging something like this could be for a Sunbeam, how it could cloud his relationship with the Church. She talked to Daniel each Sunday for two weeks after this happened, telling him she loved him, that he was a good boy, that she was glad he came to Church.

And the other women helped too.

Daniel went crazy whenever he saw that man (thankfully, always across a room or far down the hallway) for about six months after that day. Sometimes, he'd cry, "Please don't leave me, don't leave me!" Sometimes, he'd be belligerent and angry, "NO, MOM. I'M NOT GOING ANYWHERE. I HATE CHURCH!" Sometimes, he'd get overly silly and fall to the ground, out of control with giggles.

I wasn't always around when these potential interactions occurred. When I wasn't, I'd often hear about one of these women, helping Daniel get to where he couldn't see that man. They, too, took time in those succeeding months to show their love, giving him hugs, making sure he wouldn't run into J, and I'm sure, keeping him in their prayers.

This was an event that I wouldn't wish on anyone. I worry about this man's family. In my more Christlike moments, I worry about this man. But I am grateful that I got to see women who weren't afraid to speak out when something went wrong.

VESTMENTS OF THANKSGIVING
Linda Hoffman Kimball

MY UNOFFICIAL CALLING was "Nativity Exhibit Tsarina." I was the head of the ward's holiday effort in north suburban Chicago to coordinate a diverse and appealing exhibit of nativity sets from around the world. Part of this task involved contacting other churches in the area with the invitation that their members, too, would loan their sets to the exhibit. We hoped it would grow into an annual community event as similar ventures had around the country.

As we expanded our community outreach, our ward was invited to participate in another ongoing event—the annual Thanksgiving Interfaith Service hosted by Christian, Jewish, and Muslim congregations in the area. The Interfaith Council had been hosting this gathering for years without our involvement. Participating in it seemed long overdue.

The Thanksgiving Interfaith Service was scheduled on an evening when the entire bishopric was occupied with other responsibilities. The bishop accepted my offer to go, which made sense since I had already contacted a number of the Christian pastors concerning the Nativity exhibit. I called the program coordinator and was told when to show up before the service and was assigned a scripture to read to the congregation.

At first I wondered whether the rest of the pastors, priests, and imams would be confused that I, the humble nativity tsarina, was representing the Mormons for this first involvement. The more I thought about it, the better I felt. Every religious community was represented by a leader. In our Church we are all simultaneously servants *and* leaders. To see an LDS woman filling the leader role that evening might be startling in a good way for us all.

All of the participants for the service—the clergy from the various churches and I—gathered in the host church's parlor for a few introductions and socializing before the service began. Shortly before we were to enter the sanctuary, we were told to "get ready." Immediately all the others started putting on their stoles, clerical gowns and the colorful accouterments of their ministries.

I looked down at my simple autumn-toned outfit and momentarily envied their robes. Then it dawned on me that I, too, was wearing priestly "vestments." Mine (hopefully) just didn't show.

I walked down the aisle with the other leaders and knew I had a right to be there. I delivered my scripture with confidence and conviction and was filled with a joyful sense of Thanksgiving.

AS A LITTLE CHILD
Suzanne Midori Hanna

WHEN I FIRST met Pat, I never dreamed she would become the perfect nursery leader. On the few Sundays that I saw her at Church, she would be on the back row, protectively clutching her coat around her, staring blankly into space. A childhood of neglect and physical torture took its toll on her mental health, and she could hardly have a conversation with others.

She was one of the "locals," as I called them. Not a Utah transplant, but a convert to the Church in an area where the divide between those from the West and those who were raised in the area could be observed in dress, type of occupation, income level, and worldview. I rarely saw any "transplant" reach out to her, but to the locals, she was part of their ward family. They understood her blank stare; they made sure her son got to church and scouts. She always had a ride to church when her emotional state would allow her to be there. Their relationship with her was natural and loving. Although her demeanor was sullen and serious, her mere attendance at church, in the absence of much interaction with others, caught my attention.

During the twelve years that I attended her ward, I witnessed an amazing transformation. After a couple of years, we didn't see Pat at church. Eventually, Pat's son graduated from high school and received a scholarship to a prestigious art institute. We were proud of him. A few years later Pat remarried. I remember people rolling their eyes and taking a deep breath when they learned she was pregnant at mid-life. Can she do this? What will become of the baby?

Pat began attending church on a regular basis. She seemed like a different person. She found a county case manager who helped her get some medication and psychotherapy to help her find some peace from the traumas that were planted in her young and innocent soul. She beat back her demons and began to interact normally with ward members. Her tiny daughter was with her each week at church and grew to be nursery age, and then graduated on to Primary.

When I was called to be the nursery leader, I had a prompting to ask for Pat as my assistant nursery leader. What unfolded in that relationship is something I will cherish forever. Pat beamed with enthusiasm as we met to plan our schedule, activities, and songs. She was so excited to be with the children each week. After a few weeks, she was able to explain how this calling was part of her life's transformation.

"I can see that this was what I missed as a child! There were no songs or playtimes, no motherly love from others around me. Now I get to have those things, every week in nursery!"

And have them she did, with gusto! She taught the children new songs; she loved playing Ring Around the Rosie; she was always organized and ready with her part of our time with the children. Watching Pat was poetry in motion for me. She didn't just fulfill her calling with immense joy, she allowed her calling to heal her wounds. It seemed that when she embraced her calling, the joy she felt ignited her whole body and you could see the spirit glowing inside her every week.

As a Western transplant to the ward myself, I knew down deep that this transformation was "no thanks to me." Had I ever spent any meaningful time with Pat during her darkest hours? Did I know her well enough to be sensitive to her needs through those blank stares? The local members kept Pat in their hearts and nurtured her in the most subtle of ways. Sometimes they would merely act as if nothing was wrong when she could barely speak while looking down or away. They checked to see about giving her a ride to church. They were good Samaritans who would not allow her to be abandoned by the side of the road.

Over the years, her attachment to them, and consequently to the Church, endured. By the time she blessed me as a nursery assistant, Pat was a loving mother, healing herself and embracing opportunities for growth. I thought of C. S. Lewis's profound observation, "It is a serious thing to live in a society of possible gods and goddesses, to remember that the dullest and most uninteresting person you can talk to may one day be a creature which, if you say it now, you would be strongly tempted to worship."[24]

PRAYING AS SISTERS
Emily Clyde Curtis

OVER THE YEARS, my mother-in-law has been Relief Society president a couple of times. Some of her most powerful experiences have come when she has gathered a group of women together to go and pray with a sister who has been going through a difficult time.

Judy felt inspired to do this for a woman who was dying, women who were struggling with grave physical or mental illness, and women going through divorce or the loss of a loved one. She'd call each woman and ask if she would like some sisters from the ward to come pray with her, and then she'd let her bishop know the plan.

They would go to the hurting sister and all hold hands. Though as the Relief Society president Judy could have been the expected choice to say the prayer, she always asked a woman in the room who had the closest relationship to the sister they were praying for. The woman would then offer a simple prayer, thanking Heavenly Father for the blessings they all had received and then, asking for the things that her friend needed.

Judy has told me the stories of these prayers and remarked on how strong the Spirit always felt when they had these prayers. One sister commented, "The women in the Church don't know their own power until they have an experience like this." Many times, the sisters she prayed for told her later that they felt that the prayers definitely had a healing effect.

Whenever Judy or one of the women who has experienced this way of praying has told me about these prayers, I feel like I can feel the Spirit in the room. I hope to participate someday (though I'd like to be one of the sisters who comes to pray, not the one who needs the prayer).

THE CALL AND THE CALLING
Amy Gelwix

AT TWENTY-TWO-YEARS-OLD I was married, had graduated from college, and recently relocated from Salt Lake City to Atlanta, Georgia. It was the first time in my life I made a permanent move outside of Utah, away from family. My husband accepted a job with Delta Air Lines, and off we went.

While I understood there were new and unique experiences to come my way, I couldn't totally comprehend their impact.

After a few months of living in a suburb of Atlanta, my husband and I decided to move to midtown for a shorter commute to both of our offices. This move included a new ward, the boundaries of which included the Atlanta airport, meaning that any member in need who flew into Atlanta contacted our ward.

My husband was called as the financial clerk, and I was called into the Relief Society presidency. The ward was incredibly diverse, providing new connections and opportunities weekly. We formed wonderful new relationships, and thus began a fresh growing experience for us as a couple.

One weekend I received a call from the bishop, telling me of a couple that had flown in from a small town in northern Utah to complete the adoption of a baby in the area. I was given their contact information and connected with them.

A couple of weeks prior to this call, I found out that my sister was expecting another baby. While my sister's first pregnancy ended in the delivery of a healthy baby boy, a few pregnancies following that birth ended in miscarriage. My family decided to hold a fast and pray that she would be able to carry this baby full-term. Each family member fasted and prayed, but unfortunately that pregnancy, along with other pregnancies to follow, ended in miscarriage.

When I first received the phone call regarding the couple coming to Atlanta and adopting a baby, it didn't seem to be anything out of the ordinary. I got the phone call because of my Church calling, and I would follow through with the couple and assist them in any way I could. It all was very straightforward.

We invited the young couple to our home for dinner, and a friendship quickly blossomed. We had a lot in common. Their experiences in trying to build their family were touching, and observing them in their anticipation of the imminent event of growing their family by one more awoke me to the tender uniqueness of what it means to create a family beyond a husband and wife. My husband and I didn't have children at that point. Those rooms in my heart hadn't yet been opened. I was naïve to the sacred love a parent holds for a child. I was beginning to learn from this couple just how much I didn't understand.

We picked our new friends up from the hospital. As this couple emerged from the hospital with their new baby in their arms—a new family, the Spirit I felt was powerful. I understood clearly why I was put in touch with this couple, and I was humbled that I was able to be a close observer to such a sacred time in a family.

As our time with this new family came to a close, I reflected on the fast and prayers I performed on behalf of my sister. I realized that sometimes the comfort we seek for others also brings answers into our own lives—answers to questions that we didn't know we had. The Lord directly answered my fast and prayers not with the answer I was hoping for regarding my sister's pregnancy, but rather in a way that brought peace in my life.

The answer wasn't that my sister needed to adopt a baby, but rather that families are constructed in a variety of ways. Some with one child, some with many, others with none. Some children are biological, some adopted; but none less special than another. I feel blessed not only to have witnessed such an intimate time for a family, but also to have it touch and strengthen me personally.

The beautiful and satisfying aspect of Church service and leadership is the absolute truth that when we serve in our callings, as in most service opportunities, we are the ones blessed to gain insight and strength into our own personal matters. We learn more by humbling ourselves and acting than we will ever learn by sitting and passively hoping.

EQUALLY YOKED
Tania Rands Lyon

HALFWAY THROUGH MY mission in Ukraine, I was transferred to the eastern edges of a newly opened city to work with a fledgling branch that had nine baptized members and an average sacrament meeting attendance of ninety to one hundred. Our missionary district consisted of only two companionships: one pair each of sisters and elders. The senior elder was Travis Genta, and we had emerged from the MTC together, which meant we had equal seniority as missionaries although I was older, more educated, and had more language and leadership experience than he did.

At that transfer he was made simultaneously and for the first time a trainer, a District Leader, and Branch President. I, too, was training again. Both of our companions were fresh from the MTC with no previous Russian language experience and were therefore severely limited in the kinds of responsibilities they could take on. Elder Genta was understandably overwhelmed. But he was also astonishingly pure-hearted, humble, and quick to earn the trust of those around him, and the partnership we forged over the next seven months is one of the great treasures in my life.

For weeks we would alternate giving talks in Sacrament Meeting, then one of us would teach the investigator Sunday School class while the other would teach the member class, then I would teach Relief Society and he would teach Priesthood. The end of church would be swirling chaos as we tried to talk with all the visitors and cram teaching visits with them into our already crowded weekly planners. It was an exhausting but heady time.

Elder Genta and I developed a deep respect for each other. I went to him with many of my problems and questions, and he came to me with many of his. We worked out issues in the branch together on the phone almost every night. I started calling on him to administer blessings for investigators and members.

The hierarchical divisions of priesthood authority I usually felt melted away into irrelevance. The priesthood became a tool we both used in a common goal: building up the Kingdom of God. I felt we were equals yoked together in the work and pulling with all our might. Who held the Priesthood didn't seem nearly as important as who used it. Our mix of mutual goals, mutual respect, and a healthy dose of humility suddenly gave "patriarchy" a very light touch indeed.

By the time I went home and Elder Genta was sent on to open a new city, many members called us the mother and father of the branch, and the praise and love that engulfed us was dizzying. My spiritual side was awed by the feeling of being an instrument in God's hands. My political side was very much aware that no other job, including those employers who explicitly embraced women's equality, had ever granted me access to such power and influence.

Near the end of my mission, my mission president confided to me in an interview that if I had been male, he would have called me to be an assistant to the president, the highest level of leadership for missionaries in the field. I knew he meant it as a profound compliment and I felt grateful, but I had no idea what to say in reply. I spent days wondering if it made me feel proud or deeply sad. I couldn't tell. In the end it didn't matter. True service is pure, no matter the title attached.

HAZEL
Jennifer Finlayson Fife

WE HAD JUST moved to Chicago and into a new ward as our three-year-old son was entering Primary. Graham had been diagnosed with autism less than a year prior, and we had left a ward where Graham's nursery experience had been stressful. Graham's difficulty with transitions and participation in group settings and his being put off by random noises and the unpredictable behaviors of peers (nursery provided plenty of those!) made our church experience more difficult and uncertain.

As we entered our new ward, I was in many ways overwhelmed with the challenges that Graham's disability brought. I was still grieving the reality of his diagnosis and fearing what it would mean for his life and ours. Like nearly all parents with children on the autism spectrum, we investigated many therapeutic approaches and pursued several, trying to give him all that might benefit his future. We also were trying to cope with the way his condition transformed ordinary tasks and activities—from shopping to brushing teeth—into adventures and ordeals that were anything but ordinary, and that required a lot of forethought and preparation. We always needed a plan B at the ready. It was too easy to overwhelm his little nervous system.

Knowing that a regular Primary class would not work for Graham, we spoke to the bishop about our situation. In his wisdom he called a teacher just for Graham so that he could, for a time, have his own primary class.

If you look around your ward, you will notice that few callings are filled with people who have much if any professional training for what they have been called to do. The kingdom of God on earth is largely staffed with on-the-job trainees, and this was no exception. Hazel was then a woman in her late fifties with grown children. She knew almost nothing about Graham's condition, but had a sincere desire to help him and a faith that the Lord would help her do it. She threw her heart into creating lessons that he might relate to, adapted her teaching of gospel principles to what he was interested in (like learning about hell), and brought him treats and other thoughtful gifts.

Hazel's time with Graham also included chasing him around the church hallways once he learned he could escape. She also said there were many times that she feared he had taken in nothing of what she had prepared that day. One could understand how that might sap a teacher's motivation to invest a lot of time into lesson preparation, but as we could see from the steady stream of new visual aids, crafts, and activities, there was no such letdown from Hazel.

Though comprehension wasn't often evident, I'm confident that Graham did take in much of what she taught. Hazel told us one week that the week prior he had responded to none of her questions and seemed to be a million miles away, but that the following week he recited everything she had taught him about and asked questions about it. This is a common feature with children on the autism spectrum. It is easy to underestimate how much they can observe and absorb while their minds seem to be on another planet.

For us, the most important thing was the way that Hazel really devoted herself to a challenging situation for which there were not many immediate rewards or recognition. It was clear to me that she loved him, and wanted to do right by this little child who was often difficult to connect with. It was also clear to me that she cared for our family. Her taking Graham for two hours each Sunday allowed us to know he was in good hands while we took a break from a challenging role and were able to enjoy lessons and discussions in adult meetings.

Hazel's selfless devotion was very needed by Graham and by us. We will always be grateful to her for the way that she showed him how much he mattered.

SHARING STORIES
Ganie B. DeHart

FIVE YEARS AGO I was called to teach Seminary. Seminary teaching is not a calling I have ever coveted, lusted after, or vaguely desired. I teach college for a living, but my experience teaching younger adolescents was limited, to say the least. In fact, I'd always found adolescents somewhat terrifying. To make matters worse, that first year the course of study was Old Testament—the volume of scripture with which I was by far the least familiar and the one year of seminary that I hadn't managed to complete when I was in high school.

To my surprise, I soon discovered that my students weren't as terrifying as I'd expected and in fact responded well to pretty much the same teaching strategies I use with my college classes—questions that couldn't be answered with "yes" or "no," invitations to express opinions, activities that required them to apply what they'd read, and lots and lots of relevant examples to support the principles in the assigned readings. I was a bit surprised at the things they claimed never to have heard of: the story of Cain and Abel, Moses in the bulrushes, the Urim and Thummim.

We forged ahead, despite the wildness and strangeness of many Old Testament stories, and they seemed to be learning

121

quite a lot. Most weeks they read the assigned chapters, did the required homework, and participated in discussions, and it was both oddly comforting to me as a teacher and mildly alarming to me as a Church member that nearly everything we talked about seemed to be news to them. But I wasn't sure to what extent any of it was making more than a superficial impact on them.

Then one week I made an accidental discovery. We were trudging through the First Book of Kings and had gotten to Elijah's smack-down with the prophets of Baal. For some reason, I decided simply to read the whole story straight from the Bible, providing running commentary as we went. We made our way through 1 Kings chapter 18 and continued into chapter 19, where Elijah flees into the wilderness and sinks into deep despair. I commented on Elijah's apparent depression—something with which most teenagers can readily identify—and then read the marvelous description of what happened next, how God was not in the wind, or the earthquake, or the fire, but "after the fire, a still small voice" (1 Kings 19:12).

When I looked up from reading, I was greeted with an uncommon sight: four high school students sitting perfectly still, totally caught up in the story, with tears in their eyes. I was abruptly reminded of the raw spiritual power of scripture—not the single verses we're so fond of quoting, but the impact of listening to entire stories, of experiencing at length the rich, poetic language of the King James Version in particular.

My students and I had started the year as relative strangers to the Old Testament, even though it's the source for so many concepts and phrases we use regularly at church ("the still small voice" among them). We all learned a great deal that year about the cultural and historical context of the Old Testament and about the characters whose stories are told in that book of scripture (favorite unfamiliar story of the year: Ehud the Benjamite—look it up if it doesn't ring a bell, and you'll understand its particular appeal to adolescent boys).

But what I remember best from that year, and what I've tried to continue as we've moved through the rest of the standard works, is the spiritual learning that came from reading whole chapters out loud together. There is profound power in effectively immersing ourselves in the stories set down so long ago by writers eager to pass along what they'd learned about God.

WELCOMING THE LITTLE ONES[25]
Linda Hoffman Kimball

MY FRIEND SUSAN Elizabeth Howe, a professor, a poet, and a playwright, created a stage production called "A Dream for Katy: A Celebration of Early Mormon Women." One of the songs features Katy being comforted and supported by a chorus of her foremothers, who sustain and counsel her as she grapples with the challenges of her young life. When I heard this song of blessing, the words and the concept resonated with me deeply.

Some years later, I became Relief Society president. One of the things I wanted to nurture was a greater sense of unity in our diverse ward. I wanted an active way sisters could participate in such a goal. My friend Susan's song came back to me. With her permission I adapted the words, and it became our Relief Society's "Little One Welcome Song." I ran my idea of singing this song to the new babies past the agreeable bishop.

We had a lot of young families in our ward—and that

meant a *lot* of new babies. We would wait for a month or two until there was a "quorum" of babies—three or more little ones—to honor. Then I sent invitations to the babies (the "old fashioned" way, by mail):

> Dear (insert baby's name),
> Please join us for about three minutes in the Relief Society room on Sunday, (date), promptly at (time). The ladies will sing a special welcome to you as you begin your life here on earth and in our ward. Feel free to bring one or both of your parents for the occasion. RSVP (or have one of your parents do this) to Linda Kimball at . . .

On the appointed Sunday we distributed copies of the adapted song to the Relief Society sisters. In came mothers, fathers, and babies—some of whom were old enough to be wriggly—and lined up in front of the class while we welcomed "the newest young singles" into our ward with Susan's modestly tweaked, heartfelt lyrics and our warmest wishes.

In retrospect, I might have edited the song to three verses instead of all four. Since it is sung to "If You Could Hie to Kolob" (hymnbook #284—a hymn with *very* long verses), the little ones sometimes got squirmy toward the end.

I'm biased, of course, but I found every three-minute session beautiful and moving. The sisters of Relief Society felt involved in welcoming the babies and honoring the parents. The ward felt more cohesive. The looks (and tears) of joy and gratitude from the moms and dads were profound, happy and holy.

Little One Welcome Song[26]
A song of blessing, guidance, and love

Sing to the tune of *If You Could Hie to Kolob*, #284

1. In the power of the spirit
We your sisters on this day
Give to your our joyful welcome
To guide you on your way.
Dear blessed, noble children
Of great vision, love, and soul,
The world, so sad and broken
Needs your gifts to make it whole.

2. Emulate Christ's loving service
Every moment of your life;
Hold His countenance before you
Through each day of joy and strife.
There is honor in your mission.
There is glory in your youth.
Seek the best in all your labors
That your life may shine with truth.

3. Many lives will be discouraged;
Many faithful hearts will fail;
Many turn from joy to pleasure;
Many hopes grow old and stale.
In such times of loss and sorrow
When the world would bring you low,
Think on this great love we bear you.
We are here to help you know

4. There is no end to virtue;
There is no end to might;
There is no end to wisdom;
There is no end to light.
There is no end to glory;
There is no end to love;
There is no end to being;
We will know them all above.

UNRIGHTEOUS DOMINION
C. S. Williams

WHAT IS A righteous response to "unrighteous dominion?" I wrestled with this question when I served as a stake Young Women president who needed to be able to work closely with the stake Young Men president. When developing a working understanding with my male counterpart (let's call him Craig) had proven impossible, at least in the short term, I realized that I needed to find a way to serve without jeopardizing the good that could and should be done for the sake of the youth of the stake.

Trusting that the Lord is in charge of His Church and that I had been called to serve the youth of the stake (as opposed to being called to serve the stake Young Men president), I decided to go forward with plans that my counselors and I could carry out on our own, with or without Craig's support. When that wasn't possible, I made sure that the stake presidency member who had been called to counsel with the stake youth leaders was always present when my counselors and I met with the stake Young Men president. (Most often his counselors were absent.) Much to my relief, I discovered that in that setting Craig was not willing to speak or act in the same high-handed way that he behaved when I met with him one-on-one or even with my counselors.

As I saw youth events unfold, I became convinced that the Lord would make up for the lack of righteous male leadership. Although it would have been easier for me and my counselors to share the planning and orchestrating of events, the youth were still served because the Lord mercifully poured out His Spirit on us.

As time went on and I continued to ignore what I felt were unrighteous words or actions from the stake Young Men president, he gradually softened. It is hard to exert power when one's attempts to do so are ignored. This was especially true in this case because, believe it or not, Craig expected to be able to manipulate me and my counselors into carrying out the plans that he had made.

It eventually became somewhat amusing, although still disturbing, to see the tactics that Craig used to undermine the plans we made and get me in trouble with the stake counselor.

Meanwhile, I prayed for the ability to forgive Craig and treat him respectfully and patiently. For the most part, I was blessed with strength beyond my own in answer to that prayer. I also gave thanks for counselors who either remained neutral or gave open support as I struggled with the obstacles that Craig imposed. One of my counselors was reluctant to see the problem until she was forced to try to work with Craig directly. After that, she was more upset than I had ever been and could not keep herself from lobbying for his release.

As it turned out, we were all released at the same time. Looking back on this experience, I wish I had prayed more for Craig directly. I also wish I had prayed more for the stake presidency at that time. Lack of righteous leadership through-out the stake was probably a bigger problem for them than it ever was for me.

"PERFECT LOVE CASTETH OUT FEAR"
(1 JOHN 4:18)
Linda Hoffman Kimball

T HE BISHOP CALLED me into his office. I was a fairly new Relief Society president so this wasn't too unusual.

"I've just heard about something that falls into your Relief Society bucket," he said cheerfully.

Jovially I countered with, "As long as it's not dressing a dead body, I'm your gal."

He looked at me, paused, and said, "Bingo!"

He then explain that a member of the Church from out of state was in the area visiting her non-member father and had been hit and killed by a car. Her father wanted her buried here and, since she'd been to the temple, it was up to me as Relief Society president to make sure her body was dressed properly in temple clothing for burial.

Panic set in. I had never had this assignment before. I'd never been near dead bodies with the exception of cautiously and at a grim distance at funerals. The whole notion made my skin crawl and my stomach somersault. It was a strong visceral response.

"No. Please. No," my inner self shrieked while my mouth opened and the words came out, "What do I need to do?"

The next day I bravely called the funeral home and spoke to the director. "The woman's body is twisted from a lifelong disability," she said. "Oh, and of course there is some 'road rash' from the accident. We'd like to have you come tomorrow morning at nine to dress her according to your religious traditions."

The next several hours I wrestled with my sense of obligation, with my strong desire to serve, with my intense internal resistance—both mental and physical. I pleaded with God to know if there was some legitimate way I didn't have to do this. Not right now. Not this time. Please, God. No.

Then I remembered that my friend Georgia who had been a Relief Society president before me said she actually found this kind of service particularly tender, sacred, and loving. Dare I ask if she would do this for me? Was I just a wimp? Was this the kind of situation I could delegate? By now I was quivering and sick with anxiety but decided that I could at least ask Georgia for advice.

As soon as she heard my voice Georgia swooped in with comforting words and the promise that she would be more than happy to take care of this for me. She called another friend of ours, Nedra, who also found this task serene and uplifting. These two angels ministered not just to the departed sister but to me in my hour of panicked need.

Buoyed by the support and sustaining of these good sisters and all the other women who loved, taught, served, and shared in Relief Society I was able to grow in ways I never could have comprehended in those early months. In fact, two years later one of my dearest friends had a fatal recurrence of breast cancer after twenty years in remission. As her friend, as her sister, and as her Relief Society president I had the privilege of helping her closest family dress her body. It was, in fact, sacred, serene, tender, and overwhelmingly infused with love.

SETTING UP CAMP
Nancy Harward

PRESIDENT PETERSON WAS talking with someone in the hallway outside the stake offices, so as I was about to pass by, I simply smiled a greeting at my former comrade-in-arms rather than interrupt with an audible hello. But then President Peterson reached out and caught me by the arm.

"Don't go away," he said. "I need to talk to you."

Larry Peterson and I had never lived in the same ward, but after serving together as seminary teachers and then in the stake youth program for many years, we knew each other well. Perhaps too well, because that morning I was pretty sure I knew exactly what he needed to talk to me about. So as I stepped across the hall to the drinking fountain to give him a chance to finish his conversation, I tried to decide how to respond when he asked if I would consider going to Young Women camp one more time.

My service as a camp leader had begun seven years earlier, when the ward Young Women president thought it a shame not to put the early-morning seminary teacher to good use during the summer. Two years later, camp became my primary responsibility when I was relieved of my seminary assignment and called as a counselor in the stake YW presidency. The year after that, when the two stakes in our area (North and South) were reorganized to create a third, I became a counselor to the new East Stake's YW president, who was perfectly happy to leave camp in my care.

For a couple of weeks after the reorganization, I operated on the assumption that because the two original stakes' plans for that year's YW camp were already well underway and the execution date not too far off, we would just proceed as planned: the units that had formerly belonged to the North Stake would go to one camp, and the units that had been in the South Stake would go to another. We who were now in the East Stake could then wait until after that year's muddy socks and stinky T-shirts had been washed to begin worrying about creating a camp program of our own.

However, the East Stake presidency was not operating on the same assumption. They felt it was important for the members of our new stake to begin bridging the North/South divide with some unifying activities. What better place for us to learn to pull together than at the East Stake's very own YW camp? What better time than now?

Few women who had been involved in the planning of either of the two original stakes' camp programs were now in the East Stake's YW organization. Our challenge was to reconfigure the pieces we had left to fit the huge gaps created by our new situation. This meant not only finding a dozen more women who were willing and able to serve as camp leaders that summer, but also finding another venue that could accommodate us. We had three months.

Fortunately, we also had Larry Peterson, who was now the counselor over the youth programs in the East Stake presidency. Larry understood that three months wasn't much time to put together another camp staff and come up with an entirely new program, so even though the stake presidency was busy trying to hold up our end of Zion by hammering our new stake into solid ground, Larry made YW camp a priority. "Tell me who you need," he had said, so we made up a list and gave it to him. Within two weeks—unprecedented speed— the stake presidency had approved and Larry had called a new YW camp director, an activities director, three age-group leaders, a lifeguard, and a nurse.

Meanwhile, after days of Internet searches and frantic phone calls, I had determined that there was no camp facility within three states that wasn't already booked for the whole summer. However, I knew that the 4-H camp that I had previously reserved for the North Stake had enough cabins to accommodate both our groups concurrently, so I contacted the North Stake's new YW leaders and convinced them to let us use half of their venue. We'd have to share the lodge, the pool, and other common areas, but if we carefully coordinated our schedules we could stay out of each other's way. The situation wasn't ideal, but we were confident that we could make it work.

Our plans were coming together, but with only a month before camp was set to begin, we still didn't have a cook. (Neither did the North Stake. The marvelous woman who had been our cook for the past several years—the one who had not only fed the young women but taught them how to create cinnamon rolls from scratch and bake them to perfection in a Dutch oven—had moved to a distant state.) Both sisters whose names we had submitted to President Peterson as potential cooks had turned him down. We submitted another name; still no luck. Three or four names later, he finally found someone who agreed to take on the task—a woman I didn't know. When I called to introduce myself and thank her for accepting the assignment, I learned that she had never been to YW camp before. I sincerely hoped she knew what she was getting into.

Happily, Larry Peterson knew what all of us were getting into. As a veteran of numerous Boy Scout camps, he could anticipate many of our physical needs. Because we were a new stake, we owned no camping equipment other than that possessed by the individual units. Larry helped us assess what was available to borrow and what we would need to buy, and then negotiated an increase in our camp budget so the stake Young Women could begin building our own collection of tarps, washtubs, and semi-sharp knives.

The day we left for camp, he and Jay Martin, our equally valiant high council adviser, were onsite before the YW leaders, ready to help us unload our gear. The truckload of split logs they had a feeling we might need was already stacked near the fire pit. Two days later, after one of the men Jay had recruited for "priesthood duty" returned home and reported that campers were complaining about going hungry (with good reason, I should add), Larry showed up before breakfast with ten dozen blueberry muffins to supplement the Rice Krispies and Froot Loops the inexperienced cook had been serving us. It wasn't the last unexpected but very welcome delivery he would make during our sojourn in the wilderness.

I will leave more detailed descriptions of that week at camp to your imagination, stating only that while most of its elements could have used some refining, it also produced some nuggets of pure gold. Girls from one end of our nascent stake who had arrived carping about having to attend "someone else's camp" were throwing their arms around new friends from the other end of the stake by the time they had to go home. Leaders who had been reluctant to give up cherished traditions eagerly created different ones with their new cohort. I gained renewed appreciation for enthusiastic youth camp leaders, dedicated staff members, and supportive priesthood advisers.

Once we had processed everyone's reimbursement forms and made room in our closet to store leftover supplies, the stake YW presidency moved on to planning firesides and dinner-dances with our colleagues in the Young Men. President Peterson regularly attended our joint meetings, offering the perspective of a presiding authority when appropriate but otherwise just encouraging us to keep the welfare of our youth and the will of the Lord in mind.

Organizing the East Stake's YW camp for the following year was considerably less stressful than it had been the first time. Larry Peterson had heard that a rundown 4-H camp within our stake boundaries had been refurbished and was trying to fill open slots on its calendar, so we gladly signed up. Most of our staff agreed to come back—including the cook, who now had a better idea of how much a hundred teenage girls could consume. The new camp's proximity to a river allowed us to add canoeing to our slate of activities. (The girls loved that.) For a Laurel project, my youngest daughter prepared a thoughtful devotional program for the whole group's last evening together. I was proud of her, and proud of the other young camp leaders whose energy and spirit had made the camp sing. I could hardly wait to start planning for the next year.

You can guess what happened, of course. That September, not long after our stake youth conference was over, I was called as a counselor in our ward's new Relief Society presidency. As I attended my last stake youth leadership council meeting, I told the YW president and President Peterson that they could still call on me to help. "Really," I said. "If you have trouble finding a camp cook, just let me know."

I guess they knew I meant it, because the next May, Larry called me. "We're having trouble finding a camp cook," he said. "Are you available the last week of June?" And thus I had the opportunity to learn that preparing a week's worth of meals for a hundred girls in a makeshift outdoor kitchen—or rather, teaching a hundred girls how to prepare their own meals without a microwave, a refrigerator, or a sink—was even more exhausting than organizing the entire camp.

Larry called again the next May. "I really hate to ask you . . ." he began.

"No, you don't," I snapped. "You'd much rather ask me than ask someone else, because you know I'll say yes. Right?"

He chuckled. "I can't pull anything over on you, can I?"

So now we come back to where we began. It was May

again, and Larry had just pulled me aside in the church hallway. I had been to YW camp every summer for the past six
years. Could I take another year of such abuse? I had only a
moment to decide before Larry finished his other conversation
and turned in my direction.

"Okay, here's the deal," I said. "I'll do it again, but only
if I can stay in the nurse's cabin and not in a cabin full of
girls, because I'm getting too old to be able to get up in time
to start the breakfast fires without a decent night's sleep. And
I wouldn't mind having access to the private shower, either."

"If you'll do it," said Larry, "you can stay in any cabin you
want. Heck, I bet we could install a Jacuzzi for you, if that
would make you feel better."

"I don't need a Jacuzzi," I said. "But how about some of
those blueberry muffins?"

ORDINARY HEROES
Vicki Gustin Murphy

ALMOST THIRTY YEARS ago my husband and I left Boston
to settle in Shaftsbury, a small town in southern Vermont.
Ron was a fairly new convert who had served for a time in the
bishopric of the large Cambridge II Ward in Cambridge, MA.
I had been a counselor in the Relief Society with Liz Bingham
who was the most perfect example of a president that I could
imagine.

Being a member of The Church of Jesus Christ of Latter-
day Saints in a small branch—or "twig" as we call it—is much
different than we could ever have imagined. Our Bennington
Branch is one that has struggled since its formation. Through

the years a small band of saints has worked to build a chapel and expand it. We have fasted and prayed as a branch for sixty days (each member fasting a day or two) to increase and strengthen our members. We have had wonderful members move in, bless us greatly with their talents and their friendships and sadly move on.

Being few in number means multiple callings at the same time. The members rotate through the priesthood and auxiliary callings in the branch, serving in all of them eventually. One is released from a calling only to be immediately called to another. There is no time off for "good behavior." The branch evolves with the growing of our children, the aging of us and the excitement of each cherished new member.

There is a book written about the founding of our little town of Shaftsbury called *Ordinary Heroes*. That is how I see life in the Bennington Branch. Leadership to me is ordinary heroes who lead and teach by just showing up week after week and year after year, serving in callings and sharing heart and soul from cradle to grave. We have been blessed with opportunities to serve that we probably would never have had in a large, multi-talented ward. We're it. We're what the Lord has to work with.

The miracle is that He does. Our little branch has sent our sons and daughters out into the wide world to teach the gospel of Jesus Christ. For several years, we had more missionaries in the field than any other unit in our stake. I see the miracles that the Lord works every day.

I invite all who are too comfortable in a big ward to come to a small branch where you are counted and counted on and your talents and testimonies will be truly welcomed with open arms. Ordinary heroes are waiting for you.

THREE KINDS OF WARDS[27]
Kristine Haglund

I'VE ALWAYS FOUND it rather awkward to have to explain the terminology of "wards" and "stakes" to my friends of different faiths. But lately, I really like the connotations that are at least dimly present in the word "ward."

The usage of the term in the Church is left over from a time when civic and religious government were seamless in "Mormon Country," and the Church "ward" simply corresponded with political and administrative districts. We actually live in a place now where some neighborhoods are still known by their Ward numbers, and it has been fun to talk to realtors about whether we want to live in the "Second Ward" or the "Old Sixth Ward." (I have no idea where the new sixth ward is!)

The other context in which we most often use the word "ward" is, of course, in referring to divisions within a hospital—the maternity ward, the critical care ward, or the pediatric ward. (In newer hospitals, it seems that these divisions often have their own "wing", but we are not so far from the older usage that we don't recognize it).

I like thinking of the ward at church in these overlapping ways. There is the buzz of activity of the political ward: leadership meetings, Primary administration (always the busiest precinct!), the chatter of rushed activity planning, appointment making, and the constant hum of friendly nosiness. The hallways are crowded with campaign posters, urging attention to Enrichment Evenings, upcoming firesides, the food storage competition, or the Institute class. The choir director constantly begging us to follow our better angels and show up to practice singing, even though absolutely everyone knows the ward choir is a lost cause.

In the midst of this ward, the Relief Society President and the bishop and diligent home teachers and careful, unassuming friends see the other ward, the hospital ward. The woman with the crumbling marriage; the brokenhearted father whose son has just announced he's never going on a mission; the lonely widow; the young mother staggering to church through the haze of postpartum depression; the self-loathing gay man trying desperately to be someone else; the Beehive who just doesn't fit in and is mercilessly teased by her classmates; the fourteen-year-old who hates Scouts *and* basketball; the middle-aged woman recently diagnosed with MS; the new convert with a burning testimony and equally burning nicotine addiction. . . . It is a hard ward to walk through.

I used to wish that we could be more honest with each other, that we would be less shy about letting our wounds show at church. Sometimes I still wish this, and I treasure those moments when something breaks through from one ward to the other, when our collective eyes and hearts are opened for a moment to the suffering around us and we realize for just an eyeblink's time how desperately we need each other, how tender we ought to be.

But I've lately learned to be grateful for the buzz of the political ward, as well. I think most of us could not bear it if we saw the hospital ward steadily. It is too hard to unbandage our wounds and let others see and heal them, too hard to gaze for long at the afflictions of our dear ones. It is a sadly human necessity to retreat into the comfortable thrum of busy-ness, to attend to the mundane and unthreatening duties of Church administration, the routine of visiting teaching and visual aids and refreshments and high council talks and seventy-two-hour kits and basketball tournaments.

We long to visit that other ward and offer real comfort and have our own aches and pains tended to. But secretly, we are also glad when visiting hours are over. I think we should forgive ourselves our squeamishness and our weakness, and be grateful that a merciful God gives us so many practical tasks to distract us.

It is He, after all, whose wards we are.

ENDNOTES

1 Barbara W. Winder, interview by Susan W. Tanner, January 3, 2011, transcript, Church History Library, 1. Also, *Daughters in My Kingdom* (DiMK), 141.

2 See Matthew 20:20–27.

3 Julie B. Beck, "What I Hope My Granddaughters (and Grandsons) Will Understand about Relief Society" General Relief Society Conference, September 24, 2011.

4 2 Nephi 26:33

5 Dieter F. Uchtdorf, "Happiness, your Heritage," *Ensign*, Nov. 2008, 120; also DiMK, 112.

6 RS Minute Book, April 28, 1842, p. 35, also DiMK, p. 18

7 Thanks to Bishop Matthew Downs for pointing out the significance of this segment.

8 Russel M. Nelson, "Woman—Of Infinite Worth," *Ensign,* Nov. 1989, 22. See also Rom. 2:7; D&C 75:5, 128:12, 23; 132:19.

9 Spencer W. Kimball, "Relief Society—Its Promises and Potential," *Ensign*, Mar. 1976 and DiMK, 142, italics and "[brethren of the]" added for emphasis and clarity.

10 James E. Faust, "A Message to My Granddaughters: Becoming Great Women," BYU Devotional, February 12, 1985; edited version appearing in Ensign, September 1986.

11 Two of her five daughters died at the age of twenty-five (Emma Whitney Wells in 1878 and Martha Louise "Louie" Wells in 1887). Scandal hurt the family when John Q. Cannon divorced Elizabeth Anne "Annie"Wells one day in September 1886 and married her sister Louie the next day to avoid

prosecution for polygamy. John Q. confessed his sins at a stake conference and was excommunicated. Louie died after premature delivery of his baby the next spring. He came back into the Church and remarried Annie in 1888. Emmeline suffered from this and was also distressed that her daughter Melvina divorced her first husband and remarried a non-Mormon. However, the sisters supported each other and the three surviving daughters, Isabel Modalena "Belle"Whitney Sears, Melvina Caroline Blanch "Mell" Whitney Woods, and Annie Wells Cannon were all outstanding organizers, writers, and public women—correspondence from Cherry Silver summarizing from Carol Cornwall Madsen "'Granite and Old Lace': A Life sketch" in *An Advocate for Women: The Public Life of Emmeline B. Wells, 1870–1920,* (Brigham Young Univ. Press; 2006), 15–33, and also referring to "The Tragic Matter of Louise Wells and John Q. Cannon, *Journal of Mormon History* 35.2, 161–69; 178–83.)

12 Emmeline was the corresponding secretary for the General Relief Society Presidency under Zina D. H. Young (1888–1892) and general secretary under Zina D. H. Young and Bathsheba W. Smith (1892–1910). Derr, Cannon, and Beecher "Appendix: General Relief Society Presidencies and Officials, 1842–1992," in *Women of Covenant: The Story of Relief Society,* by (Deseret Book, 2002) 435.

13 Smith, *History of the Church*, 4:606 as quoted in BYU Religious Education, Religious Studies Center; Donald Q. Cannon "Joseph Smith and Agency"," in *A Witness for the Restoration: Essays in Honor of Robert J. Matthews*, ed. Kent P. Jackson and Andrew C. Skinner (Provo, UT: Religious Studies Center, Brigham Young University, 2007), 233–48.

14 Ezra Taft Benson, "Jesus Christ—Gifts and Expectations," BYU Devotional, December 10, 1974.

15 *Exponent II*, vol. 30, no. 3 Winter 2010.

16 Philip Paul Bliss, "More Holiness Give Me," *Hymns* 131, italics added.

17 Irving Berlin, *Count Your Blessings Instead of Sheep*, Irving Berlin Music Corporation, 1952.

18 From www.bycommonconsent.com, March 3, 2007.

19 Adapted from www.bycommonconsent.com on March 19, 2010.

20 Six of her nine children had died in infancy or early childhood. Godfrey, Godfrey, and Derr, *Women's Voices: An Untold History of the Latter-day Saints*, 1830–1900, (Deseret Book, 2002).

21 Ibid., 186–189.

22 Barbara W. Winder, eleventh RS general president, interviewed by Susan Tanner, January 3, 2011; transcript Church History Library, 1; *Daughters in My Kingdom*, 141.

23 *Teachings of Presidents of the Church: Joseph Smith* (2007), 451.

24 C. S. Lewis, *The Weight of Glory* (Harper Collins, 2001), 45.

25 Adapted from *Exponent II*, Volume 30, Fall 2010, 32.

26 Based on a song by Susan Elizabeth Howe, adapted with her permission, to be sung in the NS 1st Ward Relief Society, W. I. Stake. Use authorized by Bishop M. M.

27 From www.bycommonconsent.com on July 8, 2007.

Contributors

Kelly Austin
Marilyn S. Beatse
Alyson Beytien
Debra Blakely
Meghan Busse
K. Carpenter
Emily Clyde Curtis
Ganie B. DeHart
Cheryl DiVito
Cheryl McLellan Duerden
Emily Downs
Sheila Duran
Jennifer Finlayson Fife
Sherrie L. M. Gavin
Amy Gelwix
Jeanne Decker Griffiths
E. Victoria Grover
Cindy Guymon
Kristine Haglund
Suzanne Midori Hanna
Nancy Harward
Kate Holbrook
Susan Elizabeth Howe
Linda Hoffman Kimball
Lael Littke
Tania Rands Lyon
Marci McPhee
Vicki Gustin Murphy
Rebekah Neuner
Carol Lynn Pearson
Louise Plummer
Steffani Raff
Kathryn Soper
Connie Susa
Mendy Waits

About the Author

A CONVERT TO THE Church, Linda Hoffman Kimball lives in the Wilmette Illinois Stake and the Kamas Utah Stake. She holds a BA from Wellesley College and an MFA from Boston University. She is an editor and monthly blogger for the LDS women's literary website Segullah.org and writes a column for the quarterly women's journal, *Exponent II*. She is a big fan of family history research and loves to make messy art. She and her husband Chris are the parents of three remarkable adult children and the grandparents of two (so far) of the world's best grandchildren.